ALLIES IN MINISTRY

How Men Can Support Women in God's Mission

ROB DIXON

Academic
An imprint of InterVarsity Press
Downers Grove, Illinois

InterVarsity Press
P.O. Box 1400 | Downers Grove, IL 60515-1426
ivpress.com | email@ivpress.com

InterVarsity Press® is the publishing division of InterVarsity Christian Fellowship/USA®. For more information, visit intervarsity.org.

Cover design: Faceout Studio, Molly von Borstel
Interior design: Daniel van Loon
Images: © CAlexio via Shutterstock

ISBN 978-1-5140-1258-1 (print) | ISBN 978-1-5140-1259-8 (digital)

Printed in the United States of America ♾

Library of Congress Cataloging-in-Publication Data
Names: Dixon, Robert (Robert Ford), 1972- author
Title: Allies in ministry : how men can support women in God's mission / Rob Dixon.
Description: Downers Grove, IL : IVP Academic, [2026] | Includes bibliographical references and index.
Identifiers: LCCN 2025042580 (print) | LCCN 2025042581 (ebook) | ISBN 9781514012581 paperback | ISBN 9781514012598 ebook
Subjects: LCSH: Group ministry | Women in church work | Men in church work | Church personnel management | Man-woman relationships–Religious aspects–Christianity
Classification: LCC BV675 .D585 2026 (print) | LCC BV675 (ebook)
LC record available at https://lccn.loc.gov/2025042580
LC ebook record available at https://lccn.loc.gov/2025042581

33 32 31 30 29 28 27 26 | 13 12 11 10 9 8 7 6 5 4 3 2 1

"Rob Dixon is a champion for women in leadership, and he has written another practical resource for churches and leaders. Every faith community should read and use this book."

Heather Matthews, author of *Confronting Sexism in the Church*

"*Allies in Ministry* offers a thoughtful, sober reflection and inspired pathway forward for men supporting women. I found myself longing for more of this kind of embodied partnership."

Dorina Lazo Gilmore-Young, author of *Redeemer: God's Lovingkindness in the Book of Ruth*

"Rob Dixon has done it again with this mission critical, biblically grounded, and accessible guide to fostering equitable, hospitable environments where women and men can lead together, freely and fully. His seven-step pathway and stages of allyship meet men wherever they are on the journey, offering practical, Spirit-led steps that can be readily adapted to diverse ministry contexts. Rob's call to deeper partnership, accountability, and authentic transformation is both invitational and challenging—an essential resource for catalyzing liberating, Christlike change in the church today."

Liz Testa, director of equity-based hospitality and women's transformation and leadership for the Reformed Church in America

"I admire how Rob Dixon's work integrates Scriptural foundations with contemporary evidence. It is an honest conversation that prioritizes unity and hopeful possibility rather than casting judgment. Rob writes with an appropriate balance of tenderness and firm conviction, providing space for reflection and application. This book is a win for the kingdom, and the church will benefit when individuals read this book and implement the truths that are unpacked about God's original intent for women and men in ministry and the unique opportunity men are given to serve as allies to women."

Carla Working, director of clergy care and development for The Wesleyan Church

"How can Christian men elevate and honor women, coming alongside them as egalitarian collaborators for a gender-inclusive church and society? Look no further than Rob Dixon's powerful *Allies in Ministry*. Dixon leverages evidence from Scripture and his own in-depth qualitative interviews with ministerial leaders to show men the pathway to stronger leadership, humble allyship, and Christlike partnership with women in the ministry."

Brad Johnson and David Smith, coauthors of *Good Guys: How Men Can Be Better Allies for Women in the Workplace*

FOR GARRETT GIRARD

CONTENTS

INTRODUCTION

In the end, it took about three months to make the moment happen. Upon learning that his senior pastor, Rev. Lee, was starting a preaching team, my colleague Jose, who served as an associate pastor at the church, decided he would advocate for our gifted friend Nicole to have a spot on the team, with her permission.[1] Because there was no history of women preaching in their church, it took time and effort to convince Rev. Lee to extend an invitation to Nicole. To that end, Jose and Rev. Lee debated the theological questions about women preaching, and Jose was intentional about establishing Nicole's preaching history and qualifications. Ultimately Jose prevailed, and Nicole joined the team. When her time came to preach, Nicole would become the first woman to do so in their church's history.

Eventually the day came, and Nicole stood up in the pulpit, ready to preach. Before she started, however, Rev. Lee had something to say. Glancing down at his notecards, Rev. Lee began by laying out Nicole's preaching credentials, and then he prayed for her, saying, "God, we thank you so much for this time. What an awesome woman this is. Use Nicole powerfully and wonderfully to teach us."

But he wasn't done. After vouching for Nicole's skills and gifting and praying over her sermon, Rev. Lee went one step further, talking about how he was personally looking forward to learning

---

[1]I have opted to use pseudonyms throughout this book. The stories are real, but the names have been changed to shield the identity of the individuals involved.

from Nicole's message. Following this, he turned to the congregation and said, "I know a woman preaching can be a point of contention, but I want to invite us to focus on the message that God has for all of us, as God uses both men and women to speak to his people and to teach his people."

Let me tell you about the impact of Rev. Lee's introductory words that Sunday morning. At one level, what a blessing for Nicole to receive his affirmation before stepping into the pulpit for the first time. At another level, his exhortation to the community positioned them to receive Nicole's teaching well. Further, if congregants had concerns about a woman preaching, Rev. Lee's affirmation meant they would need to come to him and not Nicole if they felt the need to process their dissonant experience during the sermon.

Now consider Jose's actions behind the scenes. First, he'd engaged with Nicole about the possibility of serving on the preaching team, and he'd received her blessing to advocate with Rev. Lee for a spot on the team. Next, he'd graciously but relentlessly pushed for Nicole's inclusion on the preaching team, and he was ultimately successful. But he didn't stop there. He also walked Rev. Lee through the nuances of what to say to the congregation before Nicole's sermon. The pastor was the one who framed Nicole's speaking slot that morning, but at least in part, his notecards were full of Jose's words.

I am happy to report that Nicole shone that morning. Her sermon was a real gift to her church. And slowly but surely, the church has been moving in the direction of embracing the full leadership of women alongside men. Supported by the actions of Jose and Rev. Lee, Nicole's preaching has helped catalyze that shift, and may it continue in that congregation.

This is a book about male allyship. To be specific, it aims to articulate a pathway for developing more Christian men into more effective allies to women in their ministry contexts. As the above story illustrates, men choosing to operate as allies to women can help the church become a community where women can thrive alongside men in equal measure.

ALLYSHIP AS A CONCEPT

The word *ally* comes from the Latin word *alligare*, which means "to bind, [or to] fasten."[2] *Ally* has a robust literary track record. For example, the term appears seven different times in Geoffrey Chaucer's 1386 epic *The Canterbury Tales*, and in 1847 Alfred Tennyson used the term in his poem *The Princess*. While at points throughout history the term has been used in the context of marriage, *ally* has most often appeared in the political and military arenas as a way to describe one nation coming to the aid or defense of another nation that is under some sort of threat. For instance, Winston Churchill famously noted the importance of allies, saying, "There is at least one thing worse than fighting with allies, and that is to fight without them."[3]

Over time, the notion of allyship has been lifted from the political and military context and applied to the social arena to describe the dynamics of those with power and privilege coming to the aid of those on the margins. In particular, *ally* has broken through in the context of the LGBTQ+ conversation. It is difficult to pin down the exact moment when the term became commonly used, but it is possible that it began with the actions of a woman named Jeanne Manford. In 1972, after her gay son was attacked because of his sexuality, Manford cofounded Parents and Friends of Lesbians and Gays (PFLAG), an organization that empowers LGBTQ+ allies. For her efforts, Manford was awarded the 2012 Presidential Citizens Medal.[4]

To be sure, the term *ally* can raise objections. For instance, the fact that the term has historically been associated with a militaristic

---

[2] "Ally," in *The Oxford English Dictionary* (repr., Oxford University Press, 1961), 1:243. The *Oxford English Dictionary* also notes French term *alier* as a root.

[3] See "Winston Churchill Quotes," Lib Quotes, https://libquotes.com/winston-churchill/quote/lbm2i7u, which attributes the quote to "Lord Alanbrooke's diary, 1 Apr. 1945."

[4] See "Our History," PFLAG, https://pflag.org/our-history/.

context can render it distasteful for some people. Similarly, the term's association with the LGBTQ+ community can make it unpalatable for some people, particularly those who are cautious of an embrace of the gay community for whatever reason. Third, some argue that allyship perpetuates social divisions, noting that an ally never really becomes a member of the marginalized group they intend to support. In the end, I choose to employ the term *ally* in this book simply because I find it to be the most effective term to describe the dynamics I discuss. As readers explore the term in the context of this book, I trust it will shed at least some of its potential negative connotations.

MALE ALLYSHIP DEFINED

With this etymological context in view, I will articulate a working definition of the concept of male allyship. To generate that definition, I surveyed a range of sources from the secular arena on the topic of allyship, ultimately resulting in a composite definition that will undergird the rest of this book.[5] Four core concepts emerged from my literary review—namely, privilege, empathy, systemic engagement, and internal development.

First, the idea of privilege is recurring theme in the allyship literature. For instance, in her book *Becoming an Ally*, educator and community developer Anne Bishop defines an ally as "a member of a dominant group who works to end a form of oppression which gives them privilege."[6] I will use the term *privilege* often throughout this book. This term has been described as "an invisible package of unearned assets that [a person in a privileged group] can count on cashing in each day, but about which [they were] 'meant' to remain oblivious. . . . Privilege is like an invisible weightless knapsack of

[5]These sources come from the secular arena because there are very few sources that approach the topic from a faith-based perspective. I am happy for *Allies in Ministry* to shift that reality.

[6]Anne Bishop, *Becoming an Ally: Breaking the Cycle of Oppression in People* (Fernwood, 2015), 134.

special provisions, maps, passports, codebooks, visas, clothes, tools and blank checks."[7]

As with *ally*, *privilege* is a word that has its challenges. As a term often used in the context of diversity, equity, and inclusion conversations, *privilege* has come under fire in some venues. I opt to use the term *privilege* in *Allies in Ministry* primarily for two reasons. First, at some level, the conversation about male allyship in the church is in fact a conversation about diversity, equity, and inclusion, and so it makes sense to use terminology associated with that larger discussion. Second, I have yet to find a more compelling term, though I have certainly been on the lookout. For instance, I was recently in a conversation with a male pastor in which we explored the possibility of using terms such as "presumed legitimacy" or "implicit advantage" as synonyms. It may well be that at some point we will need to retire the term *privilege* from our collective vocabulary. Until then, my practice is to note that it can be a controversial term, define it quickly and succinctly, offer a string of practical examples, and then introduce a more colloquial expression such as "the playing field tilts in favor of men."

A second theme in the allyship literature is empathy. In her book *How to Become an Ally*, advocate Melinda Briana Epler notes, "Allyship is empathy in action. It's really seeing the person next to us—and the person missing who maybe should be next to us—and first understanding what they're going through, then helping them succeed and thrive with us."[8] Epler breaks down empathy into two components: insight and engagement. She writes, "Gaining insight

[7]This quotation comes from Peggy McIntosh's seminal article on white privilege, but I have universalized her description for the purposes of this definition. See McIntosh, "White Privilege: Unpacking the Invisible Knapsack," *Peace and Freedom Magazine* (July/August 1989): 10-12, https://nationalseedproject.org/Key-SEED-Texts/white-privilege-unpacking-the-invisible-knapsack.

[8]Melinda Briana Epler, *How to Be an Ally: Actions You Can Take for a Stronger, Happier Workplace* (McGraw Hill, 2022), 2.

includes seeing the other person's world and understanding their feelings, cognitively and emotionally. . . . Engagement [is] appreciating their unique experience without judgment and communicating this understanding."[9] Without question, successful allies clothe their allyship work in empathy.

Third, a recurring theme in the literature is that allies pursue systemic change, as opposed to solely focusing on individuals. Writing in her book *Better Allies*, leadership coach Karen Catlin notes, "Active allies utilize their credibility to create a more inclusive workplace where everyone can thrive, and they find ways to make their privilege work for others."[10] In filling out her thinking, Catlin distinguishes between knights and allies, with the difference being that allies push for systemic change, while knights swoop in to save a person or two and then leave. She writes, "In business, we don't need knights in shining armor, but we do need allies to take action and be ambassadors for change. How will you make sure you're acting as an ally, not a knight? What systemic changes can you institute to create more inclusive workplace cultures—not just for a marginalized individual or two, but for all?"[11] Catlin goes on to articulate a collection of what she calls "allyship roles," which include scholar, confidant, amplifier, sponsor, champion, upstander, and advocate.[12] Chapter four will take a closer look at each of these allyship roles.

Finally, almost every source discussed the importance of an ally doing their own inner work as a way to both process their privilege and check their motives. For example, workplace diversity consultants W. Brad Johnson and David G. Smith define a male ally as

---

[9]Epler, *How to Be an Ally*, 85.

[10]Karen Catlin, *Better Allies: Everyday Actions to Create Inclusive, Engaging Workplaces* (Better Allies, 2019), 18.

[11]Catlin, *Better Allies*, 36. In chapter six I will have more to say about how men can avoid the knight-in-shining-armor trap.

[12]Catlin, *Better Allies*, 18-27. As I will discuss throughout the book, one of the strengths of the term *ally* is that is broad enough to encompass a variety of discrete actions or behaviors.

someone who is "committed to building relationships with women, expressing as little sexism in their own behavior as possible, understanding the social privilege conferred by their gender, and demonstrating active efforts to address gender inequalities at work and in society."[13] Johnson and Smith's idea of allyship helpfully points out that male allies focus on their intrapersonal experience in addition to taking actions to affect others at both interpersonal and systemic levels.

For the purposes of this book, I will borrow components from the thinking of each of these writers and define a male ally as *a man who is engaged in an active process of understanding his privilege and empathetically seeking to leverage that privilege to benefit women both interpersonally and systemically.* This composite definition of male allyship will frame the rest of the content in this book.

MALE ALLYSHIP IN THE BIBLE

Though each of the above sources comes from the secular arena, the notion of male allyship is also a theme embedded throughout in the Bible. The presence of this theme is noteworthy given the patriarchal, even misogynistic, context in which the Bible is situated. In her book *Malestrom*, Carolyn Custis James puts it this way: "Patriarchy is not the Bible's message. Rather it is the cultural backdrop that sets off in the strongest relief the radical nature and potency of the Bible's gospel."[14] Three samples—one from the Old Testament, one from the Gospels, and one from the first church—will serve to trace the subtle but important theme of male allyship throughout the Scriptures. Further, I will use each sample to demonstrate at least one aspect of our working definition above.

---

[13]W. Brad Johnson and David G. Smith, "How Men Can Become Better Allies to Women," *Harvard Business Review*, October 12, 2018, https://hbr.org/2018/10/how-men-can-become-better-allies-to-women.

[14]Carolyn Custis James, *Malestrom: How Jesus Dismantles Patriarchy and Redefines Manhood*, rev. ed. (Zondervan, 2022), xxxvii.

First, the Old Testament law articulates a clear call for men, holders of the vast majority of cultural power in Bible times, to serve as allies to widows. The book of Ruth gives us the most helpful window into how the Old Testament law was designed so that powerful men would provide for these vulnerable women. Ruth is the star of the book that bears her name, but Boaz is an important character as well, and on two occasions his choice to obey the Old Testament law to care for widows results in provision for Ruth and for her mother-in-law, Naomi. Twice, then, Boaz takes on the identity of an ally, leveraging his privilege to benefit women in his context.[15]

As a wealthy landowner, Boaz would have been required to permit marginalized individuals, including widows, to glean food from his fields. This mandate is articulated several times in the law, including in Deuteronomy 24:19-21:

> When you reap your harvest in your field and forget a sheaf in the field, you shall not go back to get it; it shall be left for the alien, the orphan, and the widow, so that the LORD your God may bless you in all your undertakings. When you beat your olive trees, do not strip what is left; it shall be for the alien, the orphan, and the widow.
>
> When you gather the grapes of your vineyard, do not glean what is left; it shall be for the alien, the orphan, and the widow.

Ruth 2 demonstrates that Boaz adhered to this particular law, as Ruth and others glean in his fields, and yet his allyship efforts did not end there. In Ruth 2:8-9, Boaz says to Ruth, "Now listen, my daughter, do not go to glean in another field or leave this one, but keep close to my young women. Keep your eyes on the field that is being reaped and follow behind them. I have ordered the young men not to bother you. If you get thirsty, go to the vessels and drink

---

[15]It is worth noting that not only is Naomi a window, but she's also a Moabitess. So, Boaz's allyship is technically intersectional in nature. My research on male allyship did not include an exploration of intersectional realities, but such a study would be a welcome addition to this conversation.

from what the young men have drawn." It is commendable that Boaz cares for widows by keeping the law, but his allyship to Ruth is further expressed in the extra actions he takes to physically protect her and to ensure that she gets the food she needs for herself and for Naomi. In her book *The Gospel of Ruth*, Carolyn Custis James describes Boaz as "driven—you might even say obsessed—to come up with ways of making [Ruth's] mission possible. . . . Boaz extends his hand and his resources to ensure Ruth's success."[16]

The text also tells us that Boaz is related to Naomi's deceased husband, Elimelech, and this affords Boaz a second opportunity to express allyship through obedience to the law. To be specific, he is in a position to serve as a kinsman-redeemer to Ruth and Naomi. The kinsman-redeemer statute required a male relative to help preserve the family line of the deceased relative by purchasing the man's land and marrying his widow in an effort to produce a male heir.[17] Once again, Boaz steps into the ally role, ultimately becoming a kinsman-redeemer for Naomi as well as a husband to Ruth.[18] As one commentator notes, "The benefits of God's gracious providence in the mind of the author of Ruth are linked with the person of Boaz, the kinsman-redeemer, through whom these benefits in larger measure come."[19]

The book of Ruth ends by emphasizing the significance of all that has happened, including Boaz's two choices to function as an ally to Ruth and Naomi, when we learn in Ruth 4:17 that Ruth and Boaz's son Obed becomes part of the genealogy of David and, ultimately, of Jesus. Looking back at our working definition, male allyship

---

[16]Carolyn Custis James, *The Gospel of Ruth: Loving God Enough to Break the Rules* (Zondervan, 2008), 103.

[17]Leviticus 25 articulates the kinsman-redeemer regulations, and Genesis 38:8 provides another example of the law put into effect on behalf of a widow.

[18]As the text makes clear, Boaz is actually not the closest person who can make this claim, something he acknowledges in Ruth 3:13. Once the person with a closer claim opts out, Boaz fulfills the requirement.

[19]David Atkinson, *The Message of Ruth: The Wings of Refuge*, The Bible Speaks Today (InterVarsity Press, 1983), 106. The Old Testament kinsman-redeemer provides an early allusion to the ultimate kinsman-redeemer, none other than Jesus himself.

involves empathetically leveraging privilege to benefit women, and Boaz is a vivid example of this reality. Further, in this case, male allyship opens the door for God's larger mission to be fulfilled.[20]

Moving to the New Testament, Jesus embraces the allyship articulated in the law and exemplified by Boaz. I will place examples of Jesus serving as an ally to women in his ministry on center stage in chapter four, but for now consider Mark 14:3-9. In the story, a woman finds and anoints Jesus ahead of his looming crucifixion.[21] As a part of that process, she breaks open an expensive alabaster jar of perfume, drawing the ire of those gathered in the home. Their objection revolves around the fact that the perfume could have instead been used to raise money to care for the poor. It is worth noting that their objection is sensible; after all, the text tells us that the jar of nard was worth more than three hundred denarii, or about a year's worth of salary.

As those gathered in the room begin their critique, Jesus makes his allyship move in Mark 14:6-9, saying,

> Let her alone; why do you trouble her? She has performed a good service for me. For you always have the poor with you, and you can show kindness to them whenever you wish, but you will not always have me. She has done what she could; she has anointed my body beforehand for its burial. Truly I tell you, wherever the good news is proclaimed in the whole world, what she has done will be told in remembrance of her.

Note how Jesus expresses allyship in these verses. First, he validates the woman's actions in his empathetic, public defense. Second, he

---

[20]Considering the reality that the book of Ruth ultimately directs the reader to Jesus, Dorina Lazo Gilmore-Young writes, "Jesus is the grand finale of the story. Ruth, Naomi, and Boaz have pointed like arrows to his coming throughout all four chapters of their story. God reclaimed their lives, and he continues to reclaim yours and mine." Gilmore-Young, *Redeemer: God's Lovingkindness in the Book of Ruth* (InterVarsity Press, 2025), 167.

[21]This woman is unnamed in Mark's account of the story, but the parallel text in John 12:1-8 identifies her as Mary.

rebukes those who choose to critique her actions. Finally, he offers that honoring word at the end, noting that this woman will be remembered throughout history—and she has been! Reflecting on Jesus' actions in this passage, one commentator writes, "Jesus rushed to Mary's defense. Instead of condemning her, [those watching] should have commended her. Her action of anointing Jesus with a bottle of expensive perfume was a beautiful expression of her love and devotion to him, and she should not be berated."[22] Our working definition notes that a male ally's actions benefit women both interpersonally and systemically, and we see that in this story. Not only is the woman personally defended in real time, but Jesus also promises that history will confirm her actions as laudable. Again, as we will see in detail in chapter four, Jesus made a habit of operating as an ally to women in his context.

Finally, we can trace the theme of male allyship into the first church, and there is no greater example than the apostle Paul. Readers might find themselves pausing after reading this sentence, because in some circles Paul has been interpreted as being a misogynist, based largely on several passages in the epistles that temporarily restrict the full participation of women in ministry. While texts such as 1 Timothy 2:11-15 require careful interpretation, understood in context, they actually align with Paul's identity as a male ally, and in that way he follows the examples of both Boaz and Jesus.[23] Indeed,

---

[22]Walter Wessel, "Mark," in *The Expositor's Bible Commentary*, ed. Frank E. Gaebelien (Zondervan, 1984), 8:756.

[23]There are several passages in the Pauline epistles that call for contextualized, temporary prohibitions on the leadership of women in the life of the community. First Timothy 2:11-15 is one such text. In that passage, Paul exhorts his protégé Timothy to command the women of the Ephesian church to silence. While we don't know the precise reason for Paul's injunction, "it is probably because some of [the women] have been so terribly deceived by the false teachers, who are specifically abusing [them]." Until the Ephesian women were able to learn the gospel truth with greater accuracy and clarity, they were to be silent. This restriction should be understood as specific to the Ephesian church instead of normative for the church in all times. Gordon Fee, *1 & 2 Timothy and Titus*, Understanding the Bible Commentary Series (Baker Books, 1988), 73.

an examination of the final chapter in Paul's letter to the church in Rome provides a compelling snapshot of his practices of allyship. Of the twenty-nine individuals referenced in Romans 16, ten are women. Paul specifically mentions Phoebe, Prisca, Mary, Junia, Tryphaena, Tryphosa, Persis, Rufus's mother, Julia, and Nereus's sister.

It is significant that Paul names these women in this public letter. In doing so, he confers his apostolic authority on them, thus validating their ministry. How would the Roman church know of Phoebe's status as a benefactor and deacon (Romans 16:1-2)? Paul told them. How would they know that Junia is "prominent among the apostles" (Romans 16:7)? Paul told them. How would they know that Persis has "worked hard in the Lord" (Romans 16:12)? Paul told them. The Roman church, and the church universal, know about these women of valor because Paul chose to express his allyship by naming them in his letter.[24] As Susan Mathew notes, "Because the women mentioned in this list have favourable descriptions that echo Paul's of his male associates (and even of Paul himself), I will argue that these women held influential positions in the church and were responsible for the leadership of Christian communities."[25] By choosing to leverage his privilege to promote women in Romans 16 and elsewhere, Paul demonstrates his identity as an ally and once more confirms our working definition. We will see Paul's commitment to allyship for women in his context in various places throughout this book.

---

[24] "Women of valor" is a term employed by Rachel Held Evans in her book *A Year of Biblical Womanhood*. The book recounts Evans's attempt to literally live out the Bible's commands for women for an entire year, and the "woman of valor" term comes from her engagement with the text about an unnamed woman in Proverbs 31. In the end, Evans writes, "The Proverbs 31 woman is a star not because of what she does but how she does it—with valor. So do your thing. If it's refurbishing old furniture—do it with valor. It it's keeping up with your two-year-old—do it with valor. If it's fighting against human trafficking . . . leading a company . . . or getting people do your work for you—do it with valor." Rachel Held Evans, *A Year of Biblical Womanhood: How a Liberated Woman Found Herself Sitting on Her Roof, Covering Her Head, and Calling Her Husband "Master"* (Thomas Nelson, 2012), 95.

[25] Susan Mathew, *Women in the Greetings of Romans 16.1-16: A Study of Mutuality and Women's Ministry in the Letter to the Romans* (Bloomsbury Academic, 2013), 4.

Boaz, Jesus, and Paul serve as examples of male allies in the Bible. These three men embody the definition of a man who is engaged in an active process of understanding his privilege and empathetically seeking to leverage that privilege to benefit women both interpersonally and systemically. As our faith communities build a church that values the full and equal partnership of women and men in the work of ministry, would-be male allies would do well to follow their examples.[26]

OVERVIEW OF THE MALE-ALLYSHIP PATHWAY

What would it look like practically for the church to develop more men into more effective allies to women? In pursuit of answer to this question, I embarked on a qualitative research process, gathering data from a diverse sample of male leaders serving in churches and parachurch organizations. I conducted twenty semistructured interviews and three focus groups, and I ran an online survey that generated some thirty responses. The aim was to discern and articulate a developmental pathway that faith communities can use in the male-ally development process. After looking for themes and patterns, a seven-step pathway emerged.[27] *Allies in Ministry* will cover each step in the following chapters, but I provide a brief overview here.

First, would-be male allies begin from some location on a continuum of starting positions. On one end of the continuum, they might be predisposed positive to the idea of becoming an ally. On

[26]In *Allies in Ministry*, I am choosing to use the phrasing "women and men" instead of the more conventional "men and women." This choice constitutes one small effort to level out the rhetorical playing field.

[27]This pathway was originally published in *Priscilla Papers*. See Rob Dixon, "Raising Up Allies: A Standardized Pathway for Developing Men into Allies to Women," *Priscilla Papers* 34, no. 3 (2020), www.cbeinternational.org/resource/raising-allies-standardized-pathway-developing-men-allies-women/. It is worth noting that there are other ally-development models on offer. One example is Melinda Briana Epler's "stages of allyship" model, in which allies evolve through seven phases: denier, observer, learner, ally, advocate, accomplice, and activist (*How to Be an Ally*, 196).

the other end, they might be adversarial to the idea. Or, right in the middle of the continuum, they might be neutral, hovering somewhere in between. How a man starts his journey on the pathway can influence whether he will be able to progress through the remaining stages.

Next, potential allies have at least one disruptive encounter with the notion of male privilege. Disruptive encounters are experiences that provoke a reconsideration of how the world works and, specifically in this context, how the world privileges men over women. Disruptive encounters can take a variety of forms, but the core idea is that they challenge a man's perspective on privilege in the context of gender.

The third step in the male allyship pathway is a response to these disruptive encounters. The pathway has a fork in the road at this point. If a man responds positively to the disruptive encounter, humbly embracing the idea that the world largely tilts in his favor, he is more likely to continue on to the fourth step of the allyship pathway. By contrast, if a man experiences a disruptive encounter and responds with denial, he is likely not to progress on the pathway. Generally, responding well to disruptive encounters will require assistance from more-seasoned male allies.

Fourth, after successfully responding to his disruptive encounter, men begin to make initial attempts to embody the identity of an ally. The good news is that allyship is a skill men can develop in, and that process begins in step four. Though often halting or tentative, these first steps are important, as they represent a man's first efforts to act on a newly developed conviction. As Catlin notes with her seven examples of allyship roles, there is a range of ways allyship can be expressed, but the key thing in step four is that a man begins to act on his allyship conviction.

The fifth step in the male allyship pathway involves pushback. By virtue of his initial allyship activities, a man may find himself on the receiving end of critique or some form of negative evaluation. Unfortunately, the pushback step is a second point in the pathway where men can opt out of the allyship process. But if they persevere, would-be male allies can emerge further galvanized in their allyship identity and commitment.

Provided men successfully navigate the pushback experience, the sixth step in the allyship pathway involves continued investment. In this step, a man focuses on deepening his identity as an ally by taking greater risks in his allyship activities. In addition, men in step six focus on discerning which allyship roles to adopt in various situations.

In the final step in the male allyship pathway, a man's identity as an ally is firmly established. In the habitual allyship step, expressing allyship comes naturally, seemingly effortlessly. Also, in this seventh step, a male ally intentionally looks to develop men who are further down the pathway.

Taken together, the pathway looks like figure I.1.

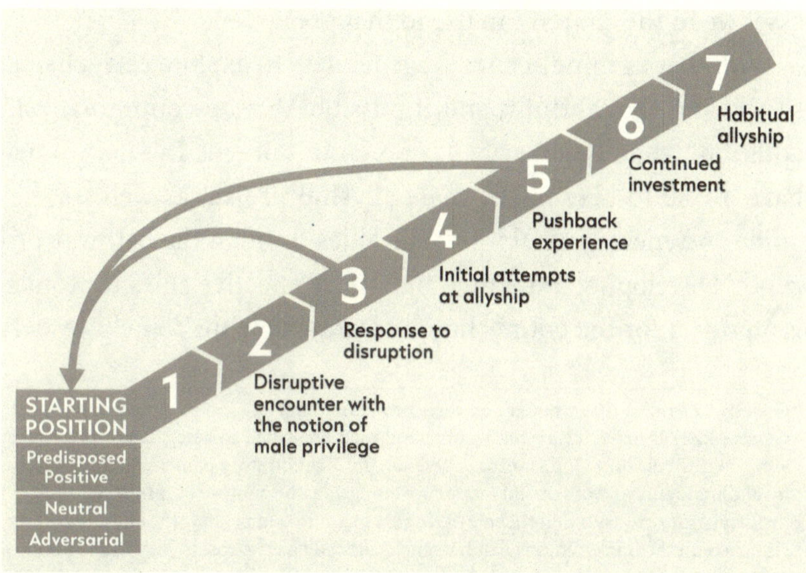

Figure I.1. Allies in ministry developmental pathway
Design credit to my dear friend (and a legitimate male ally) Adam Loveridge.

READING THIS BOOK

As noted above, I wrote this book to help the church develop more men into more effective allies to women in their contexts. After this introductory chapter, I follow the pathway articulated above, with chapters that explore each of the seven steps in the allyship pathway. Interwoven with the pathway steps are concrete suggestions for both how men can take on the identity of an ally and practical things that men can do in order to express that identity. Again, allyship is a skill that men can develop.

In the big picture, my personal passion and even my calling is to see the church embrace God's foundational vision for gender equality, namely that our faith communities would courageously embody the twin affirmations of Genesis 1 around gender, that women and men share the image of God and are called to steward God's created world in mutual and equal partnership.[28] Living into God's Genesis vision will take every tool in our collective kits, and my prayer is that this male allyship pathway will become one more asset we in the church can use to that greater end.

With that in mind, I encourage readers to explore each chapter slowly and thoughtfully, and if possible to read communally. In addition, while I primarily have men in mind as I write, women have a role to play in the male-allyship project as well, as they guide and mentor would-be male allies through the pathway process.[29] Developing more men into more effective allies to women is a project for the entire church to grapple with. To help readers

---

[28]Genesis 1:27 notes that women and men bear the image of God in equal measure, and Genesis 1:28-30 makes clear that women and men are called to coregency—that is, they are to jointly rule over God's creation. Overall, the creation story paints a picture of equality and mutuality as women and men serve alongside one another in ministry.

[29]I will have more to say about the role of women in guiding men along the allyship pathway elsewhere in the book. On one hand, women certainly have a role to play in the development of male allies, if they want it. On the other hand, there are points where doing this work can become burdensome for women, and the best approach is for more-seasoned male allies to take on this developmental work more fully.

synthesize and process what they are reading, I have included questions at the end of each chapter. May these questions guide readers' reflections, both individually and collaboratively.

QUESTIONS FOR REFLECTION

- What experiences have you had with the concept of allyship in general? With the notion of male allyship in particular?
- This chapter introduced biblical male allies Boaz, Jesus, and Paul. Can you think of other men in the Bible who function as male allies to women in their contexts?
- At first glance, where would you place yourself on the allyship pathway? Why would you place yourself there?
- Where would you place other men in your networks or faith communities?
- As you begin to explore the allyship pathway in earnest, what are your questions? What are your hopes for yourself and your faith community?

1

STARTING POSITION

THE IDIOM GOES LIKE THIS: "It's not how you start; it's how you finish."[1] Often, people use this statement to laud those who escape humble beginnings and manage to do something extraordinary with their life. It's an idea that is meant to give comfort, in the sense that anyone can overcome their past and author a brighter future.

Certainly, how or where a person finishes matters a great deal. For instance, in the context of the allyship pathway, the finished product is a man who has made a habit of thoughtfully expressing allyship in his ministry context. This man is an asset in the church's quest to become what it has always been meant to become: namely, a community in which women and men flourish together in equal and mutual partnership in ministry. As I assert in this entire book, men's developing into more effective allies to women is a crucial pursuit for today's church. The finished product is certainly important.[2]

And yet it's also true that where you start matters. Understanding a person's circumstances and context can provide guidance for

---

[1]Sometimes this maxim is phrased slightly differently: "It's not where you start; it's where you finish." Either way, the core message is the same. Determining the origin of this idiom has proved elusive, but it certainly makes appearances in a range of contexts. For instance, it is widely attributed to business guru Zig Ziglar, and the phrase features in a song from the 1973 musical *Seesaw*.

[2]Using the term "finished product" in the context of the allyship pathway is in some ways problematic for me, in the sense that male allies will forever be works in progress to some extent. Still, as step seven will attest, there is a threshold where a man comes to more fully identify as an ally to the women in his ministry context. In this way, these men do become finished allyship products.

effectively helping them change and develop. Though writing from the perspective of organizational change instead of individual change, in his seminal book *Good to Great* Jim Collins notes that organizations that become great pay careful attention to their present reality, understanding their starting position. He writes, "When . . . you start with an honest and diligent effort to determine the truth of the situation, the right decisions often become self-evident. Not always, of course, but often. And even if all decisions do not become self-evident, one thing is certain: You absolutely cannot make a series of good decisions without first confronting the brutal facts."[3] In other words, it's reckless to skip a thorough and unflinching assessment as you're getting started with something.

When it comes to the allyship pathway, knowing where a would-be male ally is starting from is crucial to helping them launch well. Indeed, how a potential male ally starts might dictate how well, or even whether, they finish.

STARTING POSITION CONTINUUM

The first step in the male allyship pathway focuses on a man's starting position relative to both an acknowledgment of male privilege and the idea of identifying as a male ally to women in ministry. My research has demonstrated that, as would-be male allies embark on their allyship journey, they are on a continuum that lays out a range of starting positions (fig. 1.1).

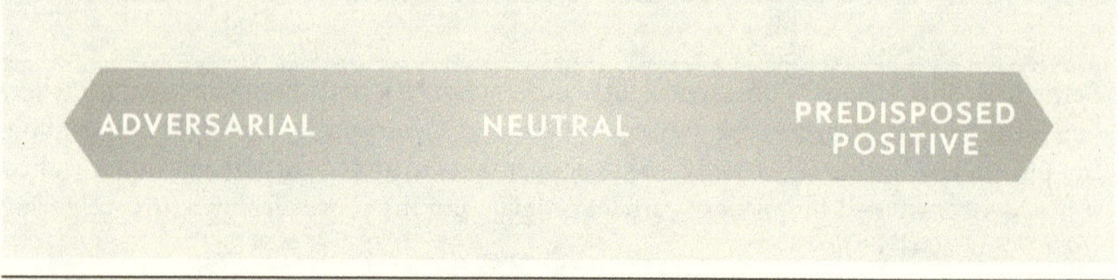

Figure 1.1. Male allyship starting position continuum

[3] Jim Collins, *Good to Great: Why Some Companies Make the Leap . . . and Others Don't* (HarperCollins, 2001), 70.

On one end of the continuum, men are adversarial toward the notions of male privilege and male allyship. For men in this starting position, there may well be an initial hostility that will need to be engaged and eventually overcome if they are going to progress along the allyship pathway.

In the middle of the continuum, men are neutral to the possibility of becoming an ally to women in ministry and to the idea of male privilege. While the neutral position was the least frequent starting position in my research on male allyship, there certainly are men who are unaware of any sort of gendered disparities in the culture and in the church, or they are intentionally neutral, not wanting to take a position for a variety of reasons.

On the other end of the continuum, men are predisposed positive to the idea of male allyship. Men on this end of the spectrum have been formed in such a way that they are open to the reality of male privilege and sensitive to the struggles that women in their networks can face in the ministry context. Generally speaking, for men in this category, the invitation to walk the allyship pathway will be an easy sell. My hunch is that many (but not all!) of the men who have picked up this book would place themselves toward the predisposed positive end of the starting-position continuum.

These are the three general starting positions, but the beauty of a continuum is that it allows for individualized nuance. For instance, men may be on the adversarial side of the continuum but not all the way out at the far edge, making them more suspicious than anything else. Similarly, men on the other side of the continuum but short of the far edge may be cautiously open instead of predisposed positive.

In this chapter I will zoom in on each of the three basic starting positions, creating a generic profile of what men in each category might have experienced and discussing why knowing a man's starting position matters as he embarks on the male allyship pathway.

One of the reflection questions at the end of this chapter will invite readers to place themselves and/or the men in their lives on the starting-position continuum, but it might also be worth doing so now as a way to enter more fully into the content of the chapter.

ADVERSARIAL STARTING POSITION

Keith is very much an ally to women in his ministry context today. As a marriage and family therapist, Keith regularly has opportunities to express allyship for women, and he is diligent and intentional about taking advantage of those opportunities. In thinking about the allyship pathway, Keith is solidly at step six and is starting to dip his toes into step seven.

That reality is a marvel considering where Keith was when he started his allyship journey. Keith grew up in an environment in which women were manifestly subservient to men, both in the home and at church. Keith's home life was marked by a strict hierarchy, with his father at the very top. When I interviewed him, Keith said, "Our lives were pretty much fully about what my father wanted to happen in any given moment." Indeed, Keith's father ruled the family home, making each of the significant (and most of the less significant) decisions. As far as Keith knew growing up, this was how it was supposed to be.

Not coincidently, Keith's family went to a church that also embraced a hierarchical reading of the male-female relationship in the Scriptures. Reflecting on his experience growing up in that church, Keith can't remember ever seeing a woman in the pulpit, as the thought that women could be pastors was anathema in his church. Because of his experience at home and in his church, Keith's first steps on the allyship pathway began from an adversarial posture. When I think about where Keith has ended up, it really does feel like a miracle.

Keith's story illustrates a few markers of a man who might enter the allyship pathway from an adversarial position, and he wasn't alone. Drawing from my research study, there are three common experiences that men on the adversarial side of the starting position continuum might have had, including a complementarian theological background, a belief in a rigid system of gender roles, and suspicion about the idea of male privilege.

Complementarian theological conviction. First, men on this side of the continuum have often been raised in a complementarian theological milieu. That is, like Keith, their default theological setting is that the Bible's message is male leadership or headship, both in the church and in the home.

In general, there are two primary ways of thinking about the Bible's message regarding women in ministry leadership, the egalitarian and complementarian positions.[4] The egalitarian theological position argues for equality between women and men both in the home and in the church, noting,

> The sexual differences that exist between men and women do not justify granting men unique and perpetual prerogatives of leadership and authority that are not shared by women. Biblical equality, therefore, denies that there is any created or otherwise God-ordained hierarchy *based solely on* sexual difference. Egalitarianism recognizes patterns of authority in the family, church, and society—it is not anarchistic—but rejects the notion that any office, ministry, or

[4]These labels define the two primary interpretative camps, but there is room for nuance as well. As with allyship-pathway starting positions, perhaps the best way to think about a theological position on women in leadership is using a continuum. In addition, theological labels such as these often need a freshening up, as the old label accrues baggage or becomes in some way insufficient. For instance, in her book *Rediscovering Scripture's Vision for Women*, Lucy Peppiatt prefers the terms *hierarchicalist* and *mutualist* instead of *complementarian* and *egalitarian*. For now, I am using the two most commonly used terms in an effort to connect to the larger theological conversation about gender partnership in the Bible. See Peppiatt, *Rediscovering Scripture's Vision for Women: Fresh Perspectives on Disputed Texts* (InterVarsity Press, 2019).

> opportunity should be denied anyone on the grounds of being male or female.[5]

In support of this nonhierarchical vision for leadership, egalitarians claim,

> Women and men are made equally in God's image and likeness (Gen 1:27), equally fallen (Rom 3:23), equally redeemable through Christ's life, death, and resurrection (Jn 3:16), equally participants in the new-covenant community (Gal 3:28), equally heirs of God in Christ (1 Pet 3:7), and equally able to be filled and empowered by the Holy Spirit for life and ministry (Acts 2:17).[6]

Egalitarians see mutuality and equality as God's design for women and men, both at home and in the church.

In contrast, the complementarian theological position argues for God-given, benevolent hierarchy.

> In the home when a husband leads like Christ and a wife responds like the bride of Christ, there is a harmony and mutuality that is more beautiful and more satisfying than any pattern of marriage created by man. Biblical headship for the husband is the divine calling to take primary responsibility for Christlike, servant-leadership, protection and provision in the home. Biblical submission for the wife is the divine calling to honor and affirm her husband's leadership and help carry it through according to her gifts. This is the way of joy.[7]

The complementarian vision for a hierarchical pattern in the marriage context extends into the church as well.

---

[5]Ronald W. Pierce and Cynthia Long Westfall, eds., *Discovering Biblical Equality: Biblical, Theological, Cultural and Practical Perspectives*, 3rd ed. (IVP Academic, 2021), 2.

[6]Pierce and Westfall, *Discovering Biblical Equality*, 2. For more information on egalitarianism, see the Christians for Biblical Equality website at cbeinternational.org.

[7]John Piper and Wayne Grudem, eds., *Recovering Biblical Manhood and Womanhood: A Response to Evangelical Feminism*, 2nd ed. (Crossway Books, 2006), 52-53.

> Paul speaks of authority and submission in 1 Timothy 2:11-12. . . . "Authority" refers to the divine calling of spiritual, gifted men to take primary responsibility as elders for Christlike, servant-leadership and teaching in the church. And "submission" refers to the divine calling of the rest of the church, both men and women, to honor and affirm the leadership and teaching of the elders and to be equipped by them for the hundreds and hundreds of various ministries available to men and women in the service of Christ.[8]

To be sure, churches and other faith communities tend to hold their theological positions on this topic differently. Some choose a less overt approach, and new attenders may go for a long time before they understand where the church is at theologically on this topic. But other churches see this as a front-burner discipleship issue and tend to be more proactive about articulating their position and its practical ramifications. Men who have been formed in a complementarian environment in which the issue is top of mind will likely start out further to the adversarial edge of the continuum, and often these men will initially find the allyship pathway to be irrelevant or even heretical.

One challenge for the project of developing more men into more effective allies to women in ministry is that the majority of Christian denominations and churches would be considered complementarian to at least some degree. Recent data from the National Congregations Study suggest that just 35.4 percent of evangelicals and 7.9 percent of Catholics believe that a woman can be a religious leader. These numbers stand in contrast to other faith traditions, including Black Protestants, 57.8 percent of whom believe women can be religious leaders, and white liberals or moderates, of whom

---

[8]Piper and Grudem, *Recovering Biblical Manhood and Womanhood*, 52-53. For more information on complementarianism, see the Council on Biblical Manhood and Womanhood website at cbmw.org.

93.1 percent endorse the leadership of women.[9] These egalitarian traditions are largely outliers. Too often, the prevailing theological wind continues to blow from the complementarian direction.

With all of this in mind, it is clear that as faith communities go about inviting men to consider embarking on a journey of becoming allies to women in ministry, they will need to discern ways to engage theologically with men like Keith, who have been steeped in complementarian ways of thinking and acting.[10]

Belief in a rigid system of gender roles. In alignment with a complementarian theological understanding, men on the adversarial edge of the starting position continuum often tend to have in mind a definitive picture of gender roles. As demonstrated in Keith's story above, for many complementarian men, male leadership is considered God's design for humanity and is thus the preferred option in any setting, at home and in the church.

For example, one complementarian scholar writes, "Alongside our insistence on women's legitimate participation in the life of the church, we need to remind ourselves again that the apostolic teaching insists on men being the primary leaders in the church (just as in marriage) and therefore excludes women from that role."[11] Practically speaking, this way of thinking tends to preclude

---

[9]"Can Women be Religious Leaders?—Belief Statistics Topic," Association of Religion Data Archives, www.thearda.com/us-religion/statistics/beliefs?qsid=4. For context, according to a 2023 Gallup survey, "About three in four Americans said they identify with a specific religious faith. By far the largest proportion, 68%, identify with a Christian religion, including 33% who are Protestant, 22% Catholic and 13% who identify with another Christian religion or simply as a 'Christian.'" "How Religious Are Americans?," Gallup, March 29, 2024, https://news.gallup.com/poll/358364/religious-americans.aspx.

[10]In my view, egalitarianism presents the best possible launching pad for effective male allyship, but it is worth considering the possibility of allyship within the complementarian construct. I do think it is possible for complementarian men to function as allies to women, but the scope will be dramatically different. Because complementarianism proposes a hierarchical system with a rigid set of gender roles, complementarian allies will be able to support women only in ministry roles that adhere to their system.

[11]George W. Knight III, "The Family and the Church: How Should Biblical Manhood and Womanhood Work Out in Practice?," in *Recovering Biblical Manhood and Womanhood: A Response to Evangelical Feminism*, 2nd ed. (Crossway Books, 2006), 352.

women from such church roles as preaching, teaching, pastoring, church planting, and providing executive leadership.

Obviously, a man who is convinced that male leadership should be normative in all situations is going to have a difficult time venturing onto an allyship pathway that has the ultimate goal of gender equality in the church. Looking ahead to step two on the allyship pathway, careful thought will need to be given regarding the potential disruptive encounters that will challenge men who hold this belief.

Suspicion regarding the reality of male privilege. Men on the adversarial side of the starting position continuum can also tend to be hesitant or even hostile to the idea that men are privileged in the culture and in the church. The idea of some sort of systematized advantage in favor of men does not compute for men in this position. More to the point, to the extent that they see privilege, they see it as God-ordained.

Because of this posture, men on the adversarial side of the starting position continuum can really struggle to be open to the idea that systemic advantage based on gender is a reality. I recall a meeting with a complementarian friend once in which he strongly disputed the concept of privilege in general, stating, "Some people just work harder and maximize their potential."[12]

Privilege, and male privilege in particular, is a real thing. The stats quoted above about the lower number of churches that affirm the full ministry of women demonstrate that for most churchgoing women, the playing field does not tilt in their favor. And while there are significant conversations worth having about just how privilege

---

[12]As I write, there is a national debate on the topic of privilege. Many on the political left argue that marginalized people face systemic injustices that must be overcome if everyone is going to be afforded equal opportunities to advance in society. By contrast, like my complementarian friend, many on the political right argue against systemic realities, instead advocating for a pure meritocracy. Men who are suspicious about the notion of privilege, then, can point to both theological and sociocultural influences.

is at work in a given situation, the fact remains that it is. For men who are unable or unwilling to engage that reality, getting started on the allyship pathway will certainly be more challenging.

Taken together, a complementarian theological position, a rigid view of gender roles with a default male leadership setting, and a built-in suspicion of the concept of male privilege present a significant adversarial trifecta. Faith communities will need to carefully and courageously engage these impediments to men entering onto the male-allyship pathway.

NEUTRAL STARTING POSITION

As I conducted my research interviews for this study, it became evident that some men are fundamentally neutral toward the idea of male privilege as well as to the possibility of embracing the identity of an ally to women in ministry. Men who are positioned toward the middle of the starting position continuum might come from a non-Christian background, might be intentionally ambivalent, and/or might be immature or unformed in their faith.

Non-Christian background. In one case, I interviewed a male ally who became a Jesus-follower later in his life. When I asked him about his starting position, he said, "Growing up an atheist, I always thought women were just as gifted as men, but it wasn't until I became Christian that I realized the great chasm between male and female leadership opportunities."[13] This surprising revelation meant this man had to play catch up to understand the different ways of interpreting the Bible on this topic.

Particularly if they have not grown up in proximity to a Christian setting, men may be legitimately unaware that this is even a

[13]This man's experience demonstrates the reality that too often secular America is ahead of the church when it comes to empowering women into service. As the Genesis 1 text so clearly articulates, women exercising leadership in full and equal partnership alongside men was God's idea in the first place. One day, I hope the church will become a leader in this area.

conversation in the church. Therefore, men in this position will require some sort of introduction to this theological debate. While the good news is that a man in this starting position is functionally a blank slate, the hard news is that it's unclear where neutral men will land once they wade into the theological waters of the conversation. Some neutral men will find themselves able and willing to venture onto the allyship pathway, but others will opt to skip the pathway altogether.

Intentionally ambivalent. Other men at this neutral starting position are there on purpose. There can be several reasons for this. First, men in this starting position may be committed to principled neutrality when it comes to theological debates. Perhaps they have had negative experiences with past theological debates that cause them to choose not to engage in subsequent conversations, or maybe they are committed to peacemaking and harmony. In either case, men in this category choose neutrality on principle.

Second, they may see the issue of women in leadership as a secondary or tertiary issue and therefore unworthy of focused reflection leading to a defined theological position. To be sure, salvation comes through Christ alone (1 Timothy 2:5), and so a person's theological position on women in leadership won't dictate whether they go to heaven. And yet labeling the topic of women in leadership a "secondary issue" can have the impact of dismissing it as an important conversation for the church to be having when the conversation is in fact crucial because it determines whether women are going to be able to use their gifts in pursuit of God's mission. Because of this, I've started referring to this topic as a 1.5 issue.[14]

---

[14]While a person's theology of women in ministry leadership is not a salvation-determining issue, it's important in a way that other theological conversations are not. For instance, a person's convictions about whether God created the world in seven days or in seven longer time periods has little impact on their day-in, day-out experience. In contrast, the issue of women in leadership has a significant impact on a person's lived experience, and that is of course especially true for women. For more on this dynamic, see chapter six.

Third, men may purposefully choose a neutral starting position because they are conflict avoidant. This choice is understandable; after all, as I've noted, the theological debate about the role of women in leadership can indeed become contentious. When conflict is a part of the experience, some men simply choose to withdraw from the conversation, embracing a neutral starting position.

Immature/unformed in faith. The goal of Christian discipleship is maturity, but sometimes men in the neutral starting position are simply not in a place where they are able to engage in a robust theological conversation that results in taking a position on the topic of women in leadership. That is, their maturity level is insufficient to permit them to have an articulated position, and they remain unformed.

I have spent my career in the college ministry context, and I can testify that many students fit in this category. It is not uncommon to have a new student say something along the lines of, "I know people and churches have different opinions on what the Bible says about women in leadership, but I'm more focused on my personal relationship with Jesus and sharing my faith with those around me." To be sure, focusing on these things is important, but at some point, people will need to wade into deeper faith discussions, including this one.

Again, my research suggests that a genuinely neutral starting position is the rarest of the three general positions, but some men certainly start their allyship journey from this position. As such, it is worth consideration as faith communities, including churches, faith-based nonprofits, and other institutions such as Christian colleges, discern ways to invite men onto the allyship pathway.

PREDISPOSED POSITIVE STARTING POSITION

I could tell from the first moment he opened his mouth that Jae was ready to set foot on the allyship pipeline. Though he had grown up in a more muted complementarian church setting, Jae quickly exhibited an openness to an egalitarian reading of the Scriptures. It was almost as if he were craving a different way of understanding the texts on this topic.

Beyond that, Jae demonstrated a deep well of empathy when confronted with the difficulties women can face in ministry. At one point, a woman on Jae's leadership team was struggling with a man in her Bible study who did not respond well to her leadership. Jae came alongside this woman, listening to her pain and gently offering guidance and advice. Around that time, I had the opportunity to talk with this woman about Jae's leadership, and she expressed profound gratitude for his pastoral care. He wasn't yet on the allyship pathway, but Jae was already beginning to use some allyship skills.[15]

Like Jae, some men are predisposed positive to becoming an ally to women in their ministry contexts. My research suggests that men in this position tend to have the following four experiences or attributes.

Egalitarian theological conviction. In the same way that a complementarian theological background can dictate the experience of men on the adversarial side of the continuum, an egalitarian theological background often marks the experience of men on the predisposed positive side of the continuum. Men with this experience have a theology that supports the full leadership of women both in the church and at home. For these men, leadership assignments are allocated by gifting and calling, not moderated by a person's gender.

In one interview, I sat with a man who had been raised in an egalitarian environment. His home church had women and men serving as copastors, and his parents sought to embody equal partnership in how they structured their marriage and family life. His

---

[15]Chapter four will lay out seven different allyship behaviors. In this vignette, Jae is using both the scholar and confidant allyship roles.

posture in approaching the allyship pathway was definitively predisposed positive, so much so that he wasn't even aware there was an alternative way of reading the Bible with regard to gender and leadership. As such, he was a good candidate for an invitation onto the allyship pathway.

Normalized experience with the leadership of women. The next chapter will explore experiences serving under the leadership of women in the context of a disruptive encounter with the notion of male privilege, but for many men on the predisposed positive side of the starting position continuum, there is a preexisting familiarity with the leadership of women in their context. Simply put, for these men, women in leadership has been a normal part of their life experience, and this makes them predisposed positive to the ideas of male privilege and male allyship. One man captured this idea perfectly in his interview, saying, "At one point, my church had three pastors, and two of them were women. And my youth director during my middle school years was also a woman. So, I was open to allyship because I was comfortable with women influencing and leading alongside men."

This experience of having seen women exercise leadership is a key part of my own allyship journey. Growing up, women carried a significant leadership role in my family's spirituality. For example, I have a clear memory of trying and largely failing to share my faith with my college roommates, only to find out my grandmother had recently led her pool cleaner to faith! Further, in the church setting, I saw models of women in leadership throughout my formational years. One of my earliest mentors was a woman named Suzy, and my church had women serving on the pastoral staff. The net result of experiencing women in leadership both at home and at church was to normalize it in my young heart and mind—of course women could serve where they were gifted and called! Because of this, the invitation to pursue male allyship was easy for me to receive.

Allyship in other contexts. A man who is predisposed positive toward becoming an ally to women in ministry might have already exhibited his allyship credentials in other contexts. In fact, these men might be familiar with the various allyship roles outlined in chapter four; they just haven't used them yet in the context of gender.

I have an online friend who serves as a pastor in another part of the country. He is a white male pastor, and I know him to be a staunch ally for our sisters and brothers of color. He does an excellent job of exposing racial injustice, often posting articles along with an exhortation for his followers to act in order to end racial oppression.[16] Not long ago, after watching him continue to express his allyship around issues of race and ethnicity, I mentioned that he might also extend his locus of concern to gender dynamics as well. Since our brief interaction, he has done so, often combining the issues of race and gender in his allyship posts.

This friend is going to always view race and ethnicity as his primary area of concern. His background makes him a motivated ally in this domain, and he feels called by God to express his allyship in this arena. But his willingness and ability to include gender in his advocacy makes the point that an ally in one context can become an able ally in another context. So, men who consistently and effectively function as allies in other contexts might well be predisposed positive to the notion of male allyship on behalf of women.

Notably high concern for the marginalization of women. Our working definition for male allyship in this book includes a word about empathy, and one marker of men on the predisposed-positive side of the starting-position continuum might well be an abnormally high amount of empathy for women being

[16]This would be a good example of the amplifier allyship role. For more on this and other allyship roles, see chapter four.

marginalized in their contexts. Looking back at Jae's story, it is clear his heart was full of concern for the struggles of the female leaders in his context. And that empathetic posture caused him to be open to the notion of functioning as an ally.

I have met other men who likewise exhibit a relatively high degree of awareness about the problems women can face in their leadership contexts. In his interview, one man cited statistics about the lack of women in upper management in his firm. In another, a man told me about how the experience of watching his sisters face gendered challenges in the educational workplace had been difficult for him. When men demonstrate, either in word or action, a notably high concern for the marginalization of women, it may well be an indicator they are predisposed positive to the notion of male allyship.

These four markers—an egalitarian theological background, familiarity with the leadership of women, allyship in other contexts, and an especially high degree of concern for the marginalization of women—may serve as indicators that a man is predisposed positive to both the notion of male privilege and the possibility of entering onto the allyship pathway. Notice the word *may* in the prior sentence. Not all men who start on the predisposed positive side of the starting position will end up becoming effective allies to women. Instead, it will take purposeful and developmental work over the remaining six steps. That said, these are important metrics faith communities can look for to identify men who may be ready to start their allyship journey.

WHY THE STARTING POSITION MATTERS

Ascertaining a would-be ally's starting position is important, primarily because it can help calibrate the type or magnitude of disruptive encounter needed in step two. Chapter two will explore the concept of disruptive encounters with the notion of male privilege in detail; for now, I will establish the link between a man's starting position and what manner of disruptive encounter might be useful. Consider three different scenarios.

First, for men who are in the adversarial position specifically because of a developed complementarian theological conviction, perhaps a theologically oriented disruptive encounter would be useful. For instance, a confrontation with an egalitarian reading of the Scriptures could be wise. Alternatively, sometimes theologically minded men might actually need a disruptive encounter that is more experiential in nature, such as personally experiencing the effective leadership of a woman in some capacity.

Second, for men who are near the center of the continuum, it is possible that a less confrontational disruptive encounter might be beneficial. Perhaps someone in the neutral starting position would be helped by easing into the conversation. That could particularly be true if they are new to this topic, either because they are immature and unformed in their faith, or they have come to faith more recently.

Finally, having clarity that a man is starting from the predisposed positive side of the starting-position continuum could mean that even a simple meeting with a mentor could function as a disruptive encounter. Perhaps a man in this position won't need much at all in order to progress to the next step in the pathway. A simple word of encouragement or invitation might prove to be sufficient.

CAN MEN CHANGE?

Whatever a man's starting position, entering onto the allyship pathway will require some sort of transformation. In the case of men who are predisposed positive to becoming an ally to women in ministry, it should be easier to embrace the allyship road, but for men in the other two categories, it could be more challenging.

After all, change is hard. Plenty of writers have attested to this reality, including James Bryan Smith in his book *The Good and Beautiful God*. Smith begins the book by describing how hard it is to effect inner change, writing, "A lot of people want to change . . . but many of them do not believe it is possible. After years of trying and failing, they lead a Christian life of quiet desperation, longing for change and yet certain it will never happen. So, they sit in their pews each week, sighing silently, resigned to their fate."[17] This morose assessment speaks to the incumbent challenge as the church considers the task of developing men from adversarial or even neutral starting positions into male allies. Change often comes slowly and sometimes not at all.

On the other hand, change is certainly possible. Smith himself came to realize he could change for the better, ultimately concluding, "The problem is not that we do not want to change, nor is the problem that we are not trying to change. The problem is that we are not training. We have never been taught a reliable pattern of transformation."[18] For Smith, such a pattern includes adopting the narratives of Jesus, participating in community, and engaging in soul-training exercises, all under the guidance of the Holy Spirit.[19] Change can happen. Keith's story from earlier in the chapter reminds us of this. Men from adversarial starting positions can indeed become male allies. It just takes careful, intentional, and sustained work.

Perhaps the most compelling example of a man becoming an ally from an adversarial starting position comes from the pages of our New Testament. As noted in the introduction, a careful look at the life and leadership of the apostle Paul portrays a man who was an ally to women. Again, Romans 16 provides a list of women Paul considered to be full partners in gospel work as well as women who were worthy of his allyship.

---

[17]James Bryan Smith, *The Good and Beautiful God: Falling in Love with the God Jesus Knows* (InterVarsity Press, 2009), 19.

[18]Smith, *Good and Beautiful God*, 19.

[19]Each of these components from Smith's rubric makes an appearance in the book, most prominently in the form of the male-allyship cohort discussed in chapter seven.

In the same way that Paul was an ally to women in practice, he was likewise an ally to women in his writing. Despite texts that temporarily restrict the ministry of women for specific reasons, Paul consistently trumpets the equal partnership of women and men in his letters. This is perhaps no greater example of this than Paul's grand egalitarian statement in Galatians 3:28: "There is no longer Jew or Greek; there is no longer slave or free; there is no longer male and female, for all of you are one in Christ Jesus." As one commentator notes, "The new vertical relationship with God results in a new horizontal relationship with one another. All racial, economic and gender barriers and all other inequalities are removed in Christ. The equality and unity of all in Christ are not an addition, a tangent or an optional application of the gospel. They are part of the essence of the gospel."[20]

So, in word and in deed, Paul is one of the most prominent male allies in the New Testament. But he didn't start out that way. In fact, Paul started his ministry life as the opposite of a male ally; indeed, Paul began from an adversarial starting position.

We know from several places in the New Testament that Paul was part of the ruling religious establishment. In fact, in Acts 23:6 he identifies himself as "a Pharisee, a son of Pharisees." In Paul's day, antipathy toward women was baked into the experience of being a religious leader. As Kenneth Bailey notes, "With the passage of time and the rise of the rabbinic movement, the position of women by New Testament times was, on all levels, inferior to men."[21]

---

[20]G. Walter Hansen, *Galatians*, IVP New Testament Commentary Series (InterVarsity Press, 1994), 112.

[21]Kenneth E. Bailey, *Jesus Through Middle Eastern Eyes* (IVP Academic, 2008), 190. Bailey describes some of the writings of a Jewish aristocratic scholar named Ben Sirach. Included in Ben Sirach's writings are prohibitions against trusting women, deeding property to women, and letting women support men. To top it off, Ben Sirach writes, "Women are responsible for sin coming into the world and their spite is unbearable." This is the misogynistic milieu that Paul would have been developed in.

Sadly, we don't have a clear picture of what exactly happened to change Paul's view of women. To use the language of step two of the allyship pathway, we are in the dark about Paul's disruptive encounter. But we can surmise a couple of things, given what we know about Paul's larger conversion to faith.

First, Paul became earnest about following Jesus. Perhaps this is because of the miraculous nature of Paul's conversion story from Acts 9, in which Jesus features prominently. In fact, it is Jesus' voice that calls Paul into a process that will radically reorient his life and leadership. In the introduction to this book I have already offered a brief overview of Jesus' allyship credentials, and a deeper dive on Jesus as an ally awaits in chapter four. Because he was an ardent follower of Jesus, we can presume that Paul would become intentional about following Jesus' allyship example.

Second, Paul joined and eventually helped to shape a faith community marked by the leadership of women. While Paul was a significant force in advocating for women in the first church, he wasn't the only one. For example, when Peter stands up to deliver his Pentecost sermon in Acts 2, he is careful to cite Joel 2:28-39, where the prophet Joel quotes God, saying, "Then afterward I will pour out my spirit on all flesh; your sons and your daughters shall prophesy, your old men shall dream dreams, and your young men shall see visions. Even on the male and female slaves, in those days I will pour out my spirit." Peter's public affirmation of the prophetic ministry of women reminds us that Paul wasn't the only budding male ally in the first church; instead, Paul was a part of a company of male allies. For more reflection on Peter's journey as a male ally, see chapter two.

Though we are sadly short on details, the apostle Paul's transformation should give us hope. People can change. People do change. More to the point, men starting from an adversarial side of the starting position continuum can indeed progress and one day become habitual allies to women in ministry.

FINAL THOUGHTS

Over the years around the holidays, I've become intrigued by the story of Joseph. Mary rightly deserves the lion's share of the Christmas spotlight, but Joseph's story merits our reflection as well, particularly viewed through the lens of male allyship and the starting-position continuum.

To be sure, Joseph, as a good Jewish male, would have been initially hostile to the notion of male privilege. His first-century world clearly tilted in his favor, and he would have seen that reality as God-ordained. But then his fiancée gets pregnant, claiming her pregnancy is the result of a miracle foretold by an angel.

At this point in the narrative, it would have been altogether appropriate for Joseph to call time out on the whole relationship. The Old Testament law contains a clear prohibition on adultery. That is made plain in the seventh commandment, and then Leviticus 20 clarifies that the punishment for adultery is death. Viewed from a cultural perspective, Joseph would be expected to haul Mary before the elders in order to press charges.

But he opts not to do that. Perhaps Joseph's starting position would actually have been somewhere between neutral and the adversarial edge. At first, Joseph decides to quietly divorce Mary; Matthew 1:19 notes that he does not want to "expose her to public disgrace." Then the miraculous happens, and Joseph comes face-to-face with an angel. The theophany constitutes his disruptive encounter, and Joseph clearly receives the intended message. His resolve is cemented, his posture is changed, and from then on Joseph becomes Mary's biggest ally.

QUESTIONS FOR REFLECTION

- For men reading this, where would you place yourself on the starting-position continuum as you think about your journey on the allyship pathway? For women, how would you describe the starting position of the men around you in your life and ministry?
- Wherever your starting position, what are some of the key influences that have formed you?
- What might be needed for you to move forward from whatever starting position you are at?

2

DISRUPTIVE ENCOUNTER WITH THE NOTION OF MALE PRIVILEGE

Noel is an ally to women now, but he hasn't always been that way. Indeed, his upbringing would place him squarely in the adversarial starting position. Like Keith from the last chapter, Noel's church both preached and modeled a paradigm in which men were leaders and women served in support roles. As was also true with Keith, Noel had never heard a woman preach during his childhood; in fact, his church had never had a woman preach in its history. Further, Noel's ecclesial experience dovetailed with how things worked in his family, in which men were seen as leaders in the home, with their wives viewed exclusively as submissive partners.

Given this theological background, Noel was always going to encounter some degree of tension participating in our egalitarian college ministry community. Indeed, over the course of his four years as a student and later as a campus minister himself, Noel experienced several gut-check moments when his complementarian background was put to the test. Perhaps the most noteworthy experience of dissonance in his theological journey happened during his senior year in college, when Noel joined a group of ten students in a weeklong Bible study centered on the Bible's message of gender equality between women and men.

During that week, Noel explored relevant texts in the context of communal Bible study, he wrestled with the equal partnership established in the creation story and the countercultural example of Jesus as articulated in the Gospels, and he engaged the first church's inclusive perspective and practice as described in both Acts and the Epistles. It is fair to say the egalitarian reflection that marked this week of intensive study firmly collided with the complementarian theology from Noel's upbringing. It is also fair to say that collision was challenging for him, as evidenced by late nights in the text, long walks mulling the implications of the text, and spirited conversations with both seminar leaders and peers. Noel's experience that week was deeply and fundamentally disruptive for him.

At the end of the week, Noel emerged open to embracing an egalitarian theological perspective. More to the point, he left the seminar committed to trying on an alternate way of thinking about the Bible's message regarding gender and ministry, one marked by equality and interdependence, during the coming months. After that season of experimentation, Noel eventually made the pivot to become fully egalitarian, and he stepped onto the allyship pathway. Today, Noel is on step six, focused on continued investment.

DISRUPTIVE ENCOUNTERS DEFINED

Noel's story captures the essence of the second step in the male allyship pathway, a disruptive encounter—or encounters—with the notion of male privilege. Disruptive encounters can take many forms, but their common thread is that they can catalyze a fundamental, even seismic, shift in a man's ways of thinking and acting with respect to the reality that the world tends to tilt in his favor as a man.

In his seminal work on how people change, Jack Mezirow articulates what he calls transformative learning theory, a ten-step process by which people change their mental models. The first step in Mezirow's process is labeled a "disorientating dilemma," which Kathleen Taylor has defined as "some experience that problematizes current understandings and frames of reference."[1] In this way, a disorienting dilemma creates dissonance, which can provide a useful context for perspective change to happen.

In the literature on transformative learning theory, there is a school of thought that says disorienting dilemmas are fundamentally unplanned, or serendipitous. For instance, Valerie Grabove posits, "A critical incident, which by its very nature cannot be planned, can serve as a catalyst for transformative learning."[2] I would challenge this proposition. I think faith communities can thoughtfully generate disruptive encounters for men in their midst, experiences that can move men along on the allyship pathway. Noel's story illustrates this reality, and I will offer further thoughts on how faith communities can proactively create disruptive encounters both in this chapter and in chapter eight.

Other writers have reflected on the value of dissonant experiences in the context of a change process. In their book *The Power of Moments*, Chip Heath and Dan Heath describe how singular experiences in a person's life can alter the trajectory of where that life is heading. As they note, "A defining moment is a short experience that is both memorable and meaningful."[3] For the Heath brothers, defining moments are characterized by four elements: They are elevated experiences that stand out above the everyday reality of a person's life, they spark a rethinking or reimagining of

---

[1]Kathleen Taylor, "Teaching with Developmental Intention," in *Learning as Transformation: Critical Perspectives on a Theory in Progress*, ed. Jack Mezirow (Wiley & Sons, 2000), 155.

[2]Valerie Grablove, "The Many Facets of Transformative Learning Theory and Practice," in *Transformative Learning in Action: Insights from Practice*, ed. Patricia Cranton (Jossey-Bass, 1997), 94.

[3]Chip Heath and Dan Heath, *The Power of Moments: Why Certain Experiences Have Extraordinary Impact* (Simon & Schuster, 2017), 12. The authors are careful to note that "short" can vary in length, from a minute to a month.

ourselves or our world, they occur when a person is fully engaged and at their very best, and they are fundamentally social in nature.

Interestingly, the Heath brothers also argue that defining moments can be intentionally facilitated. They write,

> Defining moments shape our lives, but we don't have to wait for them to happen. We can be authors of them. What if a teacher could design a lesson that students were still reflecting on years later? What if a manager knew exactly how to turn an employee's moment of failure into a moment of growth? What if you had a better sense of how to create lasting memories for your kids?[4]

One final question about disruptive encounters merits exploration: Are these encounters one-time events, or can they play out in a series of moments over time? For the most part, Mezirow and the Heath brothers seem to have singular experiences in mind, but they certainly make room for a compounding experience that stretches over some time. As noted by Laurent Parks Daloz, the great Nelson Mandela would make the case for a more cumulative approach.

> Reflecting on his gradual conversion to the great emancipating work of his life, Nelson Mandela [said], "I had no epiphany, no singular revelation, no moment of truth, but a steady accumulation of a thousand slights, a thousand indignities, a thousand unremembered moments produced in me an anger, a rebelliousness, a desire to fight the system that imprisoned my people."[5]

For a disruptive encounter during step two of the male allyship pathway, the fundamental dynamic is that something happens, either by accident or with foresight and either at one time or over some period of time, that causes a reevaluation of a man's default

---

[4]Heath and Heath, *Power of Moments*, 5.

[5]Laurent A. Parks Daloz, "Transformative Learning for the Common Good," in Mezirow, *Learning as Transformation*, 106.

way of thinking regarding his privilege, opening the door to further self-reflection and an openness to taking on the identity of an ally to women in the ministry context.

DISRUPTIVE ENCOUNTERS IN SCRIPTURE

The Bible is full of disruptive encounters. Time and again, characters in Scripture have their perspectives challenged, often through jarring experiences. Perhaps the most vivid example of disruptive encounter comes from Exodus 3:1-12.[6] In the passage, Moses is tending his father-in-law's flock when he encounters a bush that is burning but never consumed by the flames. Exodus 3:3 describes Moses' initial experience this way: "I must turn aside and look at this great sight and see why the bush is not burned up." As if this sight alone weren't enough to disrupt Moses' reality, once he nears the bush, God begins to speak to him from the bush, ultimately calling Moses into service as God's prophet. Throughout the text, there is this sense that something extraordinary is happening and that Moses will be unable to avoid experiencing it.

The effect of this disruptive encounter on Moses is profound, resulting in a radical reorientation of Moses' life and purpose. From that moment on, Moses becomes God's mouthpiece and God's agent sent to rescue the Israelites from captivity in Egypt.[7] Reflecting on the impact of this experience as well as other such moments in Moses' life and leadership, Ruth Haley Barton notes,

> Moses' whole life can be viewed through the lens of his private encounters with God and how his soul was strengthened through

---

[6]Moses' experience with the burning bush will take center stage in this survey, but plenty of other examples could be marshaled, including Abraham's covenantal meeting with Yahweh in Genesis 15, David's rebuke from Nathan following his transgressions in 2 Samuel 12, Zechariah's experience with Gabriel in Luke 1, and Peter, James, and John's experience at the transfiguration in Luke 9.

[7]It must be noted that ultimately Moses will require additional disruptive encounters as he lives into his prophetic calling, including later on in Exodus 3, when God reveals God's divine identity to his reluctant prophet.

> those encounters. He did not seem to have any great strategies for leadership except to seek God in solitude and then carry out what God revealed to him there. He routinely sought God out (or God sought him), there was an encounter, and then Moses did what God told him to do. For Moses, leadership was that simple.[8]

The story of Moses and the burning bush represents a general disruptive encounter, but of course it is not specifically associated with the notion of male privilege. As noted in the last chapter, upon meeting Jesus in miraculous fashion, the apostle Paul seems to have undergone a transformation regarding his view of women. The same could be said of Peter, chief among Jesus' twelve disciples. Indeed, in the Gospels the Peter goes on a journey that seems to result in his embracing a countercultural view of women.

A quick look at the Peter's experience in the book of John is instructive in this regard. In John 4, Jesus engages in conversation with a Samaritan woman at a well. In John 4:8, John lets the reader know that Jesus and the woman are alone, as his disciples, including Peter, have gone to a nearby town to buy food. What follows is a rather intense conversation, one that includes a thorough review of the woman's marital history as well as a proclamation of Jesus' messianic identity.[9]

Right at the end of their conversation, the disciples return from their errand, and John the narrator also returns to help the reader understand their reaction to seeing Jesus alone with the woman. Simply put, the disciples are aghast. In John 4:27, John writes, "They were astonished that he [Jesus] was speaking with a woman."

[8]Ruth Haley Barton, *Strengthening the Soul of Your Leadership: Seeking God in the Crucible of Ministry* (InterVarsity Press, 2008), 31. From personal experience as well as the observation of others, it seems as if any encounter with God could become a disruptive encounter of some sort.

[9]This passage will make a reappearance in chapter four in the context of various types of ally behaviors or roles. At the beginning of the story, Jesus functions as a confidant to the woman. Toward the end of the passage, when he commissions her to go to her town to tell her peers about him, he functions more as a sponsor.

Though they opt not to express their astonishment out loud, their reaction reveals their culturally conditioned view of women. Indeed, "Jewish piety warned men not to talk much with women (some rabbis added, even with one's own wife!), both because of temptation and because of what others might think."[10] It is difficult, then, to overstate how unusual it would be for Jesus have a protracted and private conversation with this woman. Along with the rest of the disciples, Peter's astonished reaction makes complete sense, given the patriarchal cultural context.

Fast-forward eight chapters to John 12, to a story I mentioned in this book's introduction, where Jesus and his disciples are in the home of Lazarus in Bethany. At dinner, Mary comes and breaks open an expensive bottle of perfume and uses it to anoint Jesus' feet. Her action draws a swift rebuke, but John is careful to explain that the rebuke doesn't come from the disciples en masse; rather, it is only Judas Iscariot who publicly laments her action. While it is possible that Peter and the other disciples agreed with Judas but chose silence, it is also possible that he was alone in his view. In contrast to Judas, perhaps Peter and others among the Twelve had arrived at a place where, like Jesus, they could judge the woman's action to be warranted and even commendable.

This idea that Peter had shifted his view of women during his time walking alongside Jesus gains further traction with a look at the scene in John 20. In the passage, Mary Magdalene goes to Jesus' grave only to realize that the stone has been rolled away and Jesus' body is missing. Her first response to this discovery is to seek out Peter, along with an unnamed disciple. When she delivers the news of the missing body, their response is not suspicion or even the astonishment they had exhibited earlier.

---

[10]Craig S. Keener, *The IVP Bible Background Commentary: New Testament* (InterVarsity Press, 1993), 274.

It is important here to note that a suspicious response to Mary's testimony would be more than warranted. Peter and the other disciple's acceptance of Mary's testimony would have confounded the first readers of the text because "most of Jesus' Jewish contemporaries held little esteem for the testimony of women; this reflects a broader Mediterranean limited trust of women's testimony and speech, also enshrined in Roman law."[11] Peter and his colleague could be excused from discounting Mary's announcement and continuing on their way.

Instead, the text says, "Peter and the other disciple set out and went toward the tomb" (John 20:3). Further, the next verse lets us know they ran there (John 20:4). This response seems to demonstrate Peter and the other disciple's changed posture toward women. In the moment, they judge Mary Magdalene's words to be credible and actionable, even worthy of haste. These men have come a long way from their astonished reaction to Jesus' conversation with the woman at the well in John 4.[12]

As with Paul's transformation regarding his view of women, we are not given specific details of what Peter's process entailed, but we do know this: Peter had spent his days in the company of Jesus, a consistent and generous ally to women. Indeed, "the prominence of women in the Gospels and Jesus' interaction with them—scandalous for an esteemed rabbi—elevates them to a new dignity amid a rigid patriarchy."[13] So we can reasonably presume that his chief follower might well have come to embrace Jesus' view of

---

[11]Craig S. Keener, *The Gospel of John: A Commentary* (Hendrickson, 2003), 2:1192.

[12]It is important to note that the Gospel accounts are not in complete harmony here. In the parallel account in Luke 24, the text specifically notes, in Luke 24:11, that after Mary Magdalene and other women inform the disciples about Jesus' resurrection, "These words seemed to [the disciples] an idle tale, and they did not believe them." The one exception in the Lukan account is Peter, who, in Luke 24:12, "ran to the tomb; stooping and looking in, he saw the linen cloths by themselves; then he went home, amazed at what had happened." While it is unclear what happens with the unnamed disciple in Luke's version of events, it is clear that Peter is the one who heeds Mary's words in both accounts.

[13]Donald Kraybill, *The Upside-Down Kingdom* (Herald, 2018), 202.

women. It seems plausible that observing Jesus interact with women was itself the disruptive encounter that catalyzed a reimagination of Peter's theology and practice regarding women.[14]

TYPES OF DISRUPTIVE ENCOUNTERS

In this second step on the allyship pathway, disruptive encounters can take a variety of forms. Some are process oriented, while others are one-off experiences. Some are overt, while others are subtle. And some are planned, while others are more spontaneous. The common thread in the context of the male-allyship journey is that these disruptive encounters challenge a man to consider afresh his experience with the notions of male privilege and male allyship. My research process uncovered seven different examples of disruptive encounters, including wrestling with Scripture, hearing evocative stories, engaging with real-world statistics, visioning for a preferred future, experiencing women in leadership, trying on a new way of thinking and operating, and observing models of male allyship.

Wrestling with Scripture. Time in Scripture can certainly function as a disruptive encounter with the concept of male privilege. Noel's story at the beginning of this chapter affirms this truth, but this aspect also came up more broadly in my research on male allyship. For instance, one man described his experience of studying the book of Mark and having the Bible study leader point out the countercultural ways Jesus interacts with women in the narrative. As this man reflected on this experience, he noted that it "opened my eyes and helped me realize that I wanted to be someone, like Jesus, who honored and elevated women."

---

[14]Keen readers will remember the reference to Peter as a budding ally in chapter one, where his Pentecost sermon in Acts 2 features a reference to the Joel 2 prophecy that both women and men will prophesy. This may well constitute further evidence of Peter's transformation regarding his view of women.

Similarly, another man had his view of women disrupted by focused time in the Scriptures, saying, "I had decided that I wanted to see women empowered and given access to power, authority, and influence. I wanted this because I was helped to interpret and understand key difficult passages related to men and women in ministry. I was helped to see in Scripture how God gifts and empowers women for ministry in his kingdom."

In Hebrews 4:12, the author notes that "the word of God is living and active and sharper than any two-edged sword, piercing until it divides soul from spirit, joints from marrow; it is able to judge the thoughts and intentions of the heart." As one commentator writes,

> The images the author employs in this marvelous passage are effective ones. Like a sharp sword which can lay open the human body with one slashing blow, so the sword of Scripture can open our inner life and expose it to ourselves and others. . . . Such honest revelation is what we need to humble our stubborn pride and render us willing to look to God for forgiveness and his gracious supply.[15]

As this short text makes clear, Scripture is essentially designed to function as a disruptive encounter in our life.

Setting aside well-curated space to do earnest reflection on the Bible's message regarding women in leadership could create an effective disruptive encounter for would-be male allies. In preparing and hosting such a time, facilitators should give careful attention to who is in the room, what is being studied, what extratextual resources are engaged, and what the overall tone of the experience is.

As I will discuss in the next chapter, Scripture is also useful in helping would-be allies respond to a disruptive encounter. But the

---

[15]Ray C. Stedman, *Hebrews*, IVP New Testament Commentary Series (InterVarsity Press, 1992), 60.

activated Scripture discussed in Hebrews can also *be* the disruptive encounter as men wrestle with God's vision for gender equality and the full partnership of women and in the work of ministry, as well as the implications for how they might steward their privilege as would-be male allies.

Hearing evocative stories. Not long ago, I got to meet a male ally named Raymond. I was introduced to Raymond by my friend and colleague Linda, who serves as a national leader in Raymond's denomination. Raymond had caught Linda's eye as an ally during a meeting when he made an observation about how there were too few women involved in leadership in a particular denominational program. His ability to see that problem, coupled with his willingness to verbalize it, screamed "ally" to Linda.

When we met, Raymond told me about his journey of becoming an ally to women in leadership. In particular, he pointed to his most transformative disruptive encounter, which consisted of an afternoon of women sharing their stories of marginalization and abuse with him. As he reflected on that experience, he noted, "It was hard to listen to their stories, but, as I listened, I could feel my heart bend toward my sisters, and I knew then that I wanted to help our organization change the way it operates, so that other women wouldn't have to have the same experience that these women did."

Stories can function as powerful disruptive encounters. In another of their books, *Made to Stick*, the Heath brothers point out that a "story's power . . . is twofold: it provides simulation (knowledge about how to act) and inspiration (motivation to act). Note that both benefits, simulation and inspiration, are geared toward generating action."[16] As would-be male allies venture in and through the second step on the allyship pathway, they will benefit

[16]Chip Heath and Dan Heath, *Made to Stick: Why Some Ideas Survive and Others Die* (Random House, 2007), 206.

from hearing well-told stories, both stories that illustrate the challenges of women in their context and stories of men who have successfully navigated the pathway and now identify as male allies. My hope is that even the stories in this book could function as disruptive encounters for male readers.

Engaging real-world statistics. Recently I was talking about male privilege with a new friend of mine, and he immediately disputed the concept, asking, "What evidence do you have that male privilege is actually a thing?" Knowing that he is a businessman who regularly deals with data and numbers, I proceeded to share some of the data presented below, and it helped open the door to a larger process of considering his privilege.

Like my friend, some men will have their worldviews challenged by statistics that illustrate the nature of the disparity of social power between women and men. Indeed, numbers and data can serve as a useful way to guide men into a disruptive encounter that demonstrates the reality of male privilege. Sadly, in an American context, there are numerous examples of statistics that could be marshaled as a disruptive encounter.[17] Here are three examples from the political, economic, and ecclesial contexts.

In the political sphere, though the numbers have been trending in the direction of greater parity, women remain underrepresented in the upper echelons of American political life. Though women constitute about 50 percent of the US population, the Center for American Women in Politics notes that as of November 2024, women make up only 25 percent of the Senate, 29 percent of the House of Representatives, 32 percent of statewide legislature seats, and 24 percent of governorships.[18] In each case, these numbers are

---

[17]If we widen the aperture to consider male privilege on a global scale, the disparity in social power becomes even wider, and thus male privilege becomes even more pronounced.

[18]"Women in Elective Office 2024," Center for American Women and Politics, https://cawp.rutgers.edu/facts/current-numbers/women-elective-office-2024.

either all-time highs or close to it. Viewed from a global perspective, this gendered political inequality is appalling; as of January 2024, the United States ranks just seventy-second on the list of women's participation in national legislative bodies.[19]

In the economic arena, it is a similar story. Though the numbers have slowly been trending in the direction of parity, women remain significantly underrepresented in most economic arenas. For example, a 2024 survey of Fortune 500 companies reveals just fifty-two women in a CEO position. That number is actually up from forty-two in 2021, but that is still just 10.4 percent overall.[20] Further, the data suggest that women own just 34 percent of small businesses in the United States. That number also represents a move in the direction of equality, but there is clearly still work to be done. Finally, the wage gap, which is defined as the difference between what a woman gets paid versus a man if they are working the same job, currently sits at 84 cents on the dollar. According to a March 2024 US Department of Labor blog post,

> *Overall, women are paid less than men.* On average, women working full-time, year-round are paid 84% of what men are paid. In other words, the typical woman working full-time would need to work from January 1, 2023, until March 12, 2024, to make what the typical man working full-time made in 2023. This wage gap also persists within all major race and ethnic groups. For instance, Hispanic women ($41,137 median annual salary) make 13% less than Hispanic men ($47,420 median annual salary). This inequity is even greater for Black and Hispanic women when compared to white, non-Hispanic men.[21]

---

[19]"Monthly Ranking of Women in National Parliaments," IPU Parline, https://data.ipu.org/women-ranking/?date_month=1&date_year=2024.

[20]"2024 Women CEOs in America Report," Women Business Collaborative, https://wbcollaborative.org/women-ceo-report/.

[21]"What You Need to Know about the Gender Wage Gap," Workplace Fairness, https://www.workplacefairness.org/what-you-need-to-know-about-the-gender-wage-gap/. Again, it is

Closer to home, the church is no stranger to a fundamental power imbalance between the genders. As noted in chapter one, complementarian theology persists as the default setting for most churches and congregants. And yet the disparity exists even in egalitarian denominations that do permit the full participation of women in leadership. For instance, a 2023 CNN article noted that the four-million-member Evangelical Lutheran Church in America, a denomination that has ordained women into pastoral leadership since 1970, reported women in just 22 percent of senior pastor positions.[22]

Well-sourced and carefully vetted statistics can invite men to reevaluate their privilege. Especially for men trained in data and analytics, statistics can give them an objective look at the reality of the gender disparities that exist in so many sectors of our society. In that way, statistics and data can function as a disruptive encounter for potential male allies.

Visioning for a preferred future. *Switch*, yet another book by the Heath brothers, was written to help individuals and organizations navigate change. *Switch* introduces a threefold change formula. To effect positive change, leaders must direct a person's rational mind, motivate their emotional center, and thoughtfully shape the situation or context in which the change is being considered. One strategy for directing a person's rational mind as well as engaging them at an emotional level is a "destination postcard." The Heath brothers write, "We want what we might call a destination postcard—a vivid picture from the near-term future that shows what could be possible."[23]

---

worth noting that there are intersectional realities to be considered in the larger discussion about privilege.

[22]AJ Willingham, "More Women Are Aiming to Become Church Leaders. Together, They Could Change American Christianity," CNN, July 30, 2023, www.cnn.com/2023/07/30/us/women-church-leadership-united-states-cec/index.html. It is worth noting that some other numbers look better for the Evangelical Lutheran Church in America. As the article notes, 46 percent of Evangelical Lutheran Church in America bishops are women, and 54 percent of assistant or associate pastors are women.

[23]Chip Heath and Dan Heath, *Switch: How to Change Things When Change Is Hard* (Crown, 2010), 76.

If compelling, destination postcards can function as a disruptive encounter for would-be male allies. In 2024, my wife, Amy, and I published a picture book titled *Penny Preaches*, about a little girl who decides she wants to become a preacher.[24] Since the book came out, we have heard from a number of women and some men about how the book represents the kind of church they long to see, one in which little girls like Penny are invited to consider how God has gifted them and how they might use those gifts in the church without limitation. In this way, *Penny Preaches* has served as a destination postcard. Other examples of destination postcards that function as disruptive encounters in this area could include:

- An elder team, church staff team, or pastoral leadership team that works hard to achieve gender parity on their team
- A leadership development pipeline that is full of both women and men, so that when leadership positions open up, there are qualified candidates from both genders to choose from
- A ministry workplace that is safe for women, where women don't have to experience marginalization or, worse, abuse
- A church that is so intentional about gender representation that every week both girls and boys can see someone that looks like them up front during the worship service

Destination postcards are essentially vision statements, and God-given vision has the capacity to disrupt a person's status quo. For would-be male allies, a compelling destination postcard can cause them to rethink their view of the world and thoughtfully evaluate their male privilege.

Experiencing women in leadership. The presence of the Holy Spirit was tangible and potent as my friend and colleague Eliza gave a call to faith at a large conference for college students.

---

[24]Amy Dixon and Rob Dixon, *Penny Preaches*, illustrated by Jennifer Davison (InterVarsity Press, 2024).

Thousands of students responded that day, many making first-time decisions to place their faith in Jesus, with many more committing to following Jesus more fully. As I sat in the back of the arena listening to Eliza deliver the most powerful call to faith I have heard in my almost thirty years of campus ministry, I couldn't help but wonder how many men were experiencing disruption as a woman stood before them speaking God's words with eloquence and passion, propelled by the undeniable presence of the Holy Spirit.

Experiencing women offering effective, godly leadership can function as a disruptive encounter for men as they start out on the allyship pathway. This is particularly true for men who might come from adversarial or neutral starting positions because the experience may create a significant level of discomfort. In my research process, respondents provided a litany of examples of contexts in which the experience of women in leadership functioned as a disruptive encounter:

- Choosing to attend a church pastored by a woman or attending a church where women would be preaching
- Enrolling in seminary classes taught by women
- Attending Bible studies facilitated by women
- Opting to consume media, including podcasts, videos, and books, created by women
- Mentoring a woman in leadership
- Being mentored by a woman in leadership

In the last chapter, I recounted a bit of my own story as someone who was predisposed positive to the ideas of male privilege and male allyship. In part, my openness was a product of this particular genre of disruptive encounter. As mentioned, I was mentored by a woman named Suzy when I was in high school, and then I was mentored by a woman named Úna when I got to college. Experiencing the effective leadership of these women in my life challenged my perspective by normalizing the idea that women could lead in the church. As my own story illustrates, the experience of witnessing women exercise capable leadership can operate as an important disruptive encounter for men as they experience step two on the allyship pathway.

Trying on a new way of thinking and operating. At the beginning of this chapter, I shared the story of Noel's disruptive encounter during the seminar focused on women in the Bible, an encounter that included his intention to try on a new way of thinking and acting. For about six months, he explored an egalitarian mode of operation, and during that time he focused on two things.

First, he chose to place himself under the leadership of women. He availed himself of many of the experiences included in the list above. Doing so provided Noel with opportunities to push deeper into the dissonance he was feeling. In the process, he explored his male privilege more fully, and it helped ready him to respond favorably to the disruption in step three.

Second, he became a "privilege detective," looking for examples of male privilege in his life and in the broader culture. I had encouraged him in this regard partly because exploring the concept of privilege was something that had marked my own journey as an ally. For about six years, I considered my own male privilege in a blog called *Challenging Tertullian*, and I posted about my discoveries on Mondays and Thursdays.[25] In the beginning, my thesis was this:

---

[25]Rob Dixon, *Challenging Tertullian* (blog), https://challengingtertullian.com/. Without question, Tertullian made some amazing contributions to the field of Christian theology. But he also had some theological clunkers, including his views of women. In one regrettable passage, Tertullian wrote to Eve, "You are the Devil's gateway; you are the unsealer of that tree; you are the first foresaker of the divine law; you are the one who persuaded him whom the Devil was not brave enough to approach; you so lightly crushed the image

> Male privilege exists in our culture and is something that benefits men like me. Since Jesus calls me to surrender everything I've got to his leadership, that's as true for my privilege as it is for my car, house, etc. And as I willfully and joyfully surrender this privilege and invite Jesus to use it, I get to see him empower the women around me and advance his mission in my context.[26]

In the end, my experience with the blog confirmed my thesis. And the process of continually reflecting on my male privilege, coupled with writing on it twice per week, represented an ongoing disruptive encounter in my life. As Noel's experience attests, following some initial dissonant experience, a process of exploration can deepen a man's understanding, open him up for ongoing transformation, and help him along the allyship pathway.

Observing models of male allyship. When I first started in full-time ministry, I was assigned to work on a campus situated in a theologically conservative community. Just about every church in our city proclaimed and practiced a complementarian interpretation of the Scriptures, which meant that our particular campus ministry community was essentially alone on an egalitarian island.

Because of this dynamic, it was not uncommon for local pastors to attempt to influence our community in this area. Sometimes those conversations were gentle and full of grace; other times, not so much. At one point, in my second year of ministry service, a local church decided to end its financial support because we had hired a woman to serve on our team. Given our long-standing partnership with this church, this was a painful experience, certainly for my female colleague but also for our whole leadership team.

---

of God, the man Adam." It is writings such as this that set up a situation in which male privilege is normative in the Christian church, so when I posted on my blog, I imagined myself sitting across from Tertullian, giving him a piece of my mind.

[26]Rob Dixon, "About This Blog," *Challenging Tertullian* (blog), https://challengingtertullian.com/about-this-blog/.

In response to this church's decision, two of the men on our team decided to go visit the church's pastor to lobby on behalf of our colleague as well as our ministry. I watched as they prepared for the conversation, reviewing the egalitarian books on their shelves as well as discussing their agenda for the conversation. As they went about their preparation, I could tell that this conversation was important to them. They took their identities as allies seriously.

Watching my male colleagues prepare to defend their sister's right to lead was an important disruptive encounter for me. In this book, I define a male ally as a man who is engaged in an active process of understanding his privilege and empathetically seeking to leverage that privilege to benefit women both interpersonally and systemically, and I saw that definition being lived out right in front of me. I remember distinctly having the realization that I wanted to follow their example one day in my life and leadership.

When more-seasoned male allies seek to proactively develop men who are further back on the pathway, their model alone can create a productive disruptive encounter.[27] After all, it is one thing to consider male allyship as a conceptual proposition; it's another thing to see it in real life. Intentional modeling can function as a transformative disruptive encounter.

FINAL THOUGHTS

In her book *Learning to Listen, Learning to Teach*, educational theorist Jane Vella reflects on a pivotal time in a class session when a student verbally disagreed with her in the middle of her lecture. She writes, "I have found that the moment of dissent in a course is a rich moment of learning for all."[28] As a part-time professor who

---

[27]Further discussion of modeling and the allyship pathway will take center stage in chapters seven and eight.

[28]Jane Vella, *Learning to Listen, Learning to Teach: The Power of Dialogue in Educating Adults*, rev. ed. (Wiley & Sons, 2002), 67.

has experienced verbal pushback in the classroom, I am certainly challenged by Vella's interpretation of that moment being a productive experience for the class!

Indeed, we tend to think of disruptions as a bad thing, as a nuisance or something to be avoided or resolved as quickly as possible. But as Vela's reflection demonstrates, disruptive encounters can actually become places of deep formation. For would-be male allies, disruptive encounters with the notion of privilege are a key step in their allyship identity journey.

QUESTIONS FOR REFLECTION

- Generally speaking, how have you seen disruption operate as a context for your personal or spiritual growth?
- What are some examples of disruptive encounters with the notion of male privilege you've seen in your life or in the life of other men around you?
- How can you and your community create disruptive encounters with the notion of male privilege for potential male allies in your life?

3

RESPONSE TO DISRUPTION

Martin was one of my favorite students to work with. He had gotten involved in our ministry during his first year on campus, and he quickly impressed me with his passion for shepherding his peers. Ahead of his sophomore year, he signed up to lead a Bible study, which meant moving back into the residence halls to meet new students. Martin served in the Bible study leader role for two years, and he did so well that our leadership team invited him to serve as our community's outreach coordinator for his senior year. He gladly accepted our offer.

I was the campus minister assigned to support the student leadership team, which put me in direct oversight of Martin's outreach ministry. What a joy it was to journey with him and to help him grow as a leader and a disciple. In particular, I helped Martin become a good friend and partner to both the women on our leadership team and the women in our community who were a part of his outreach ministry, which was no small thing given his complementarian upbringing. Like Keith and Noel from the last two chapters, Martin came from the adversarial starting position.

Even as he was engaged in leadership with our community, Martin was also involved with a local church, and that local church was vociferous about its complementarian convictions. To be specific, they preached male headship regularly in their college ministry, which is how Martin discovered texts that temporarily restricted the full ministry of women due to localized circumstances, including 1 Timothy 2:11-15.

The clash between his church's complementarian reading of the Scriptures and his egalitarian experience partnering with women in our community created a disruptive encounter for Martin. To his credit, he pressed into the tension, beginning to study the Scriptures in earnest. I remember meeting with him to process his experience with various texts on multiple occasions.

Unfortunately, in the end, Martin decided that God's intention was male headship, both in the church and in the home. This new theological conviction forced him to conclude that women and men were not designed to partner together on equal footing, and not long after this he chose to leave our ministry community. I was devastated. I was losing one of my favorite students, and we were losing a potential male ally. Martin had barely gotten started on his allyship journey, and now he was off the pathway altogether.

RESPONDING TO DISRUPTION

Following one or multiple disruptive encounters, would-be male allies face the first of two forks in the road along the allyship pathway. The options in step three are either to progress forward toward step four or to return to the starting position.

What makes that choice is how a man responds to having his view of the world challenged in the context of his disruptive encounter. If a man is able to go through that experience or experiences and respond by shifting his thinking and posture, embracing both the notion of male privilege and the journey of male allyship, he will continue on the pathway. On the contrary, if, like Martin, a man isn't able or willing to make that shift, he will opt out and return to the starting position.

RESPONDING TO DISRUPTION IN SCRIPTURE

In the same way the Bible gives us a window into what disruptive encounters can look like, we are also allowed to see how characters in Scripture respond to those encounters. And while the patriarchal culture of the day prohibits us from getting a good look at how men such as Paul and Peter responded to their disruptive encounters specifically with the notion of male privilege, we are given a window into what it can look like generally to respond to a disruptive encounter.[1] There is no greater illustration of this than in the New Testament Gospels as individuals and groups respond in various ways to the ultimate disruptive encounter: the incarnation of Jesus.

On one hand, the Bible offers plenty of stories of people who respond well to Jesus. In fact, the first person to respond well to the disruptive encounter of Jesus is his mother, Mary.[2] Most scholars think Mary would have been a teenager when she was approached by the angel Gabriel in the beginning of the Gospel of Luke. Gabriel's message is supremely disruptive; namely, Mary will become pregnant, with the Savior of the world, no less! In fact, *disruptive* is probably too mild a word for what this experience would be like for Mary. As noted previously, there could well be harmful implications for her becoming pregnant before her marriage.

---

[1]In chapters one and two, I posited that the disruptive encounter for both Paul and Peter was Jesus himself, that watching how Jesus interacted with women challenged these men to reexamine their own perspectives and practices. We might conclude that their response to this disruptive encounter was also Jesus-centric. That is, Paul and Peter responded to their disruptive encounters by spending yet more time with Jesus and with Jesus-followers. And so it should be for men on the allyship pathway. Each of the response tactics in this chapter could be couched as a way to connect more deeply with Jesus in an effort to process the experience of a disruptive encounter.

[2]Mary responds to Jesus' incarnation even before his incarnation, but other characters respond well once Jesus is present and active in ministry. The first disciples, characters such as Zacchaeus from Luke 19, and each of the women highlighted in chapter four come to mind.

> [Mary] was not yet married to Joseph. His reaction to her pregnancy might have been expected to be a strong one and Matthew tells us that he did in fact think of divorcing her (Mt. 1:19). Again, while the death penalty for adultery (Dt. 22:23f.) does not seem to have been carried out often, it was still there. Mary could not be sure that she would not have to suffer, perhaps even die.[3]

Despite the potential risks associated with her situation, to her eternal credit Mary responds well to being invited into the very epicenter of the incarnation. Her affirmative response is marked by three actions. First, Luke 1:29 tells us that Mary "pondered" and was "perplexed" by the angel's words. As we will see shortly, focused reflection, or pondering, can be a helpful tool in the context of responding to disruptive encounters for men at this step on the allyship pathway. Second, in Luke 1:34, Mary asks what can only be described as a perfectly reasonable question: "How can this be, since I am a virgin?" Along with pondering, question asking can also be an important part of the response process for would-be male allies. Finally, these two responses are followed by Mary's powerful proclamation in Luke 1:38: "Here am I, the servant of the Lord; let it be with me according to your word." Mary's openhearted posture here is noteworthy; indeed, one commentator dubs it an "exemplary attitude of servanthood."[4]

In contrast to Mary's commendable response to her disruptive encounter, there are a selection of New Testament characters who respond poorly to Jesus' incarnation. Most notably, consider the Pharisees, whose response to Jesus is suspicion, even hostility, from

---

[3]Leon Morris, *Luke*, Tyndale New Testament Commentary (Eerdmans, 1983), 74.

[4]Walter L. Liefeld, "Luke," in *The Expositor's Bible Commentary*, ed. Frank E. Gaebelein (Zondervan, 1984), 8:832. It is also worth noting that Mary's words in Luke 1:38 echo Hannah's words from 1 Samuel 1:18, in response to the prophet Eli's declaration that she will give birth to Samuel: "Let your servant find favor in your sight." These two women are models for Christians who find themselves faced with unexpected, even unwanted, callings.

the very beginning. They have already had multiple run-ins with Jesus by the time they approach him to question him about fasting in Mark 2:18-22. After parrying away their question, Jesus proceeds to issue a warning. In Mark 2:22, he says, "Similarly, no one puts new wine into old wineskins; otherwise, the wine will burst the skins, and the wine is lost, and so are the skins, but one puts new wine into fresh wineskins." Those hearing this warning would have understood and appreciated Jesus' metaphor. "Wine could be kept in either jars or wineskins; the latter would stretch. Old wineskins had already been stretched to capacity by fermenting wine within them; if they were then filled with unfermented wine, it would also expand, and the old wineskins, already stretched to the limit, would break."[5]

The implications of Jesus' words here are profound. He himself represents the fresh way of thinking about God and others; in the language of the passage, Jesus is the new wine. By contrast, the Pharisees represent the old wineskins. And, as Jesus warns, any attempt to shoehorn Jesus' new teachings into old ways of thinking about faith and religiosity will ultimately fail. Indeed, "the main teaching of the parable seems to be that the newness the coming of Jesus brings cannot be confined to old forms."[6]

Sadly, we know the Pharisees never learned the lesson of this parable. They never become the new wineskins, and once it became clear to them that the presence of Jesus was causing them to lose social and religious power, they ramped up their opposition to Jesus, right up until the cross. In stark contrast to Mary's open posture toward the incarnation of Jesus, the Pharisees chose a closed posture; in the end, the wineskins did indeed burst.

---

[5]Craig S. Keener, *The IVP Bible Background Commentary: New Testament* (InterVarsity Press, 1993), 140.

[6]Walter W. Wessell, "Mark," in *The Expositor's Bible Commentary*, ed. Frank E. Gaebelein (Zondervan, 1984), 9:637.

One challenge with using the Pharisees as a lens for evaluating the importance of responding to a disruptive encounter is that their response is clearly sinful. Jesus says as much in Matthew 23:15, saying, "Woe to you, scribes and Pharisees, hypocrites! For you cross sea and land to make a single convert, and you make the new convert twice as much a child of hell as yourselves."[7] I want to be clear: I am not saying that failing to respond positively to the notion of male privilege and opting out of the allyship pathway is automatically a sinful decision; in the end, that is up to each individual man and to God.

But I am saying that it certainly represents a missed opportunity. A man who denies the existence of male privilege and opts off the allyship pathway misses out on the chance to understand himself more clearly, to see the world as it truly is, and to participate more fully in the larger project of helping the church embody God's Genesis 1 vision for the full and mutual partnership of women and men in ministry.

So, the Gospels give us examples of both positive and negative responses to the disruptive encounter of the incarnation, and later in Mark Jesus offers insight on why people respond the way they do. In Mark 4:1-20, Jesus tells the parable of the sower. In the story, he notes that seed goes out from the sower indiscriminately. What makes the difference in whether that seed will eventually produce a crop is the state of the soil it lands on. Hard, rocky, and thorny soil won't yield fruit; instead, good, receptive soil is the only viable context for growth. Jesus clarifies this in Mark 4:20, saying, "And these are the ones sown on the good soil: they hear the word and accept it and bear fruit, thirty and sixty and a hundredfold."

As Jesus makes clear in debriefing the parable, this is a word about posture toward the new things of God. Like the good soil,

---

[7]Elsewhere, in Matthew 3:7, Jesus dubs the Pharisees a "brood of vipers."

people who have an open posture receive new teaching and respond well. There is then fruit in their lives. In contrast, hard hearts yield nothing. As one commentator notes,

> Words may be sound and lively enough, but it is up to each hearer to let them sink in and become fruitful. If [they] only hear without responding—without doing something about it and committing [themselves] to their meaning—then the words are in danger of being lost, or of never coming to anything. The whole story thus becomes a parable about the learner's responsibility, and about the importance of learning with one's whole will and obedience, and not merely with one's head.[8]

RESOURCES FOR RESPONDING WELL

Thankfully, would-be male allies have a wealth of resources to draw from in successfully processing a disruptive encounter with the notion of male privilege. During my research process, I found five different aids that men can take advantage of as they synthesize their experience; namely, safe space to reflect, focused Scripture study, deeper study, further experiences, and process helpers. In addition to having observed these five things in others, I have personally benefited from each one in my own journey through this third step on the allyship pathway.

Safe space to reflect. Again, confronted by Gabriel's declaration that she will literally bear the savior of the world in her womb, Mary's first move is to ponder the angel's words. Pondering connotes a deep, intentional level of reflection; it's more than a casual, passing thought. Indeed, the Greek word for pondering in Luke 1:29 carries the connotation of reasoning through multiple options in order to arrive at clarity. In the same way, faced with a disruptive encounter that brings the reality of male privilege into sharp relief,

---

[8]C. F. D. Moule, quoted in Wessell, "Mark," 9:651.

men will benefit from making space to intentionally ponder their experience. Doing so creates a context both to process the experience and to interact with Jesus about it.

In my own life, I wonder how many potential disruptive encounters I miss because I don't make space to ponder what I'm experiencing. Indeed, we are often too busy to carve out the space to reflect, and it will take discipline to do so. Ruth Haley Barton points to our constant need for retreat and reflection, writing, "We are distracted from our very lives; we miss out on the comfort that is there for us when we are present to our own depths in God's presence."[9]

The word *safe* in the description of this response avenue is important. It is not uncommon for men to experience pain as they process the reality of their male privilege. "When it comes to gender equality and justice, the vulnerability required of men to step back from traditional vestiges of power and to admit to complicity with privilege can be very daunting."[10] Because of this, safe space is crucial. Men should seek out unhurried, comfortable, and relationally encouraging environments as they ponder. In addition, men might benefit from pastoral process helpers and/or other resources described in this chapter.

Making space to ponder and reflect on the notion of male privilege starts with willfully setting aside time in the schedule to reflect, and then of course that space must be guarded. Once

---

[9]Ruth Haley Barton, *Invitation to Retreat: The Gift and Necessity of Time Away with God* (InterVarsity Press, 2018), 18.

[10]Don Neufeld, "Coming Alongside: Men Joining the Conversation on Equality," *Priscilla Papers* 28, no. 1 (2014): 16. Anne Bishop expresses a similar sentiment: "Coming to understand your identities as an oppressor is often an enervating process. It means being shut out from someone else's secret language; it involves accepting your inheritance of a shameful and evil past. There is guilt, which drains energy. There is always that unsettling knowledge that you cannot see what is going on as clearly as the oppressed group can. The oppressed always know a great deal more about the oppressor than the oppressor knows about the oppressed." Bishop, *Becoming an Ally: Breaking the Cycle of Oppression in People*, 3rd ed. (Fernwood, 2015), 93.

established in the calendar, there are plenty of ways to use such space and time:

- Men can make space to journal, processing their experience on paper. "On the pages of a journal, in the privacy of a moment, we can take tentative steps into truth and scour our feelings, hurts, ideas and struggles before God. . . . During times of transition, travel, loss, joy, illness, and decision making, journaling can provide a way of processing the hopes, fears, longings, angers and prayers of our heart. It can be the place we sound off before God so we don't sound off in an inappropriate way to others."[11] As noted above, disruptive encounters can produce a wide range of feelings and emotions, and journaling can create a safe context for exploring them.
- Space to reflect can involve focused prayer in response to a disruptive encounter. Engaging with God directly can open the door for greater clarity and direction. After all, God, the author of the incarnation, knows a thing or two about disruptive encounters! There is a small but important detail in the sower passage that bears note here; namely, in Mark 4:10, following the story, we learn that "when [Jesus] was alone, those who were around him along with the twelve asked him about the parables." It's the curiosity of the hearers that ultimately invokes the parable's explanation. In the same way, when men experience something that challenges their view of how the world works, they can come to Jesus in prayer, seeking fresh understanding.
- Scripture features in chapter two, in the context of functioning as a disruptive encounter, and it appears again below. Here it is important to mention that an excellent way to use time in solitude would be personal meditation in the Scriptures. As David

[11]Adele Ahlberg Calhoun, *Spiritual Disciplines Handbook: Practices That Transform Us* (InterVarsity Press, 2005), 57.

> Benner notes, "[Biblical] meditation ought to be a part of the prayer life of every Christian who seriously seeks to genuinely know God."[12]

Reflection takes work. For most men, setting aside time and space to reflect on their disruptive encounters with the notion of male privilege won't come naturally.[13] For some, even the idea of reflection might be challenging. And yet this space is crucial if men are to successfully process their experience and emerge ready to progress along the allyship pathway.

Focused Scripture study. One man I interviewed for this study evocatively described his disruptive encounter as "cataclysmic." After seeing a series of sexual-abuse statistics and hearing stories of women who had suffered abuse at the hands of powerful men, he was very open to the notion that the world tilted in his favor as a man. And yet there was still one problem for this man; namely, he needed to see this concept of male privilege played out in Scripture.

Thankfully, a male mentor in his life was ready to engage with him in focused Scripture study. Together they spent time reflecting on Philippians 2:1-11, the so-called Christ hymn.[14] In that passage, Paul notes that Jesus "did not regard equality with God as something to be grasped, but emptied himself, taking the form of a slave, assuming human likeness. And being found in appearance as a

---

[12]David G. Benner, *The Gift of Being Yourself: The Sacred Call to Self-Discovery* (InterVarsity Press, 2004), 40.

[13]Writing in the context of a marriage relationship, one psychologist puts it this way: "Men, in particular, will resist this path toward self-awareness, having a bias toward action rather than contemplation—not seeing how this process leads to a better relationship, relying on 'facts,' valuing intellect over feelings, not following through on a place to meditate, etc." Not all men are wired this way, of course, but this observation rings true generally. Catherine Aponte, "How Important Is Self-Awareness for Men?," Psychology Today, November 26, 2019, www.psychologytoday.com/us/blog/a-marriage-of-equals/201911/how-important-is-self-awareness-for-men.

[14]I am talking about this particular text in the context of men responding to a disruptive encounter, but it would just as easily function as the disruptive encounter itself.

human, he humbled himself and became obedient to the point of death—even death on a cross" (Phil 2:6-8).

Reflecting on the implications of this text for followers of Jesus, Dominique DuBois Gilliard writes,

> When we take on the mindset of Christ, we do nothing out of selfish ambition or conceit and refrain from exploiting our status and positions for selfish gain. We also, in humility, empty ourselves for the sake of the kingdom and our neighbors. This entails standing in solidarity with our neighbors when we have the option not to, placing the interests of others before our own, and prioritizing the peace and prosperity of our community above our individual success—knowing that Scripture assures us that when our communities prosper, we do as well. In taking this Christlike posture, we move toward a collectivist pursuit of freedom, flourishing, and shalom.[15]

Gilliard's reflection here helpfully positions Philippians 2:1-11 as a predicate for allyship in general and for male allyship in particular. That is, privilege is not something to be indulged for personal gain. Instead, privilege is to be leveraged for the benefit of those who are less fortunate. Indeed, by choosing to cast aside his privilege in becoming incarnate as a human and then by taking the cross, Jesus functions as the ultimate model for men pondering their male privilege.[16]

After several weeks sitting with the notion that Jesus willfully abandoned his privilege as a way to save humanity, this man was ready to fully buy in to the concept of male privilege. That focused Bible study provided the context for this man to process his disruptive encounter. As a result, he progressed along the allyship pathway into step four.

---

[15]Dominique DuBois Gilliard, *Subversive Witness: Scripture's Call to Leverage Privilege* (Zondervan Reflective, 2021), 104.

[16]The reality of this passage is that Jesus is relinquishing more than just male privilege. He is giving up nothing less than what we might call divine privilege. And if Jesus can do that, surely men can give up or leverage the social power that they/we possess.

Philippians 2 is a great place to turn in helping would-be male allies continue on the pathway following some sort of disruptive encounter, but there are others. In fact, just about any text where Jesus engages with a woman will provide an opportunity to reflect on how Jesus manages his privilege, as Jesus is continually modeling a countercultural approach to gender dynamics. One concrete place to start could be with the texts explored in chapter four.

Deeper study. Beyond Scripture study, there is a wealth of other resources that can help men process their disruptive encounter with the notion of male privilege. Making space to carefully absorb what others have said can create a helpful input stream for men as they seek to respond to their disruptive encounter. Reading alongside others in community would be even more beneficial.

After walking with a number of men through step three on the pathway, I have curated lists of resources in three categories that are germane to positively traversing step three in the allyship pathway: namely, egalitarian theology, the notion of privilege, and the concept of allyship.

Here are several resources that articulate an egalitarian theological perspective:

- *Two Views on Women in Ministry* provides a comparative look at complementarianism and egalitarianism. As noted in chapter one, these are the two primary ways of thinking theologically about the topic of women in leadership.[17]
- *Discovering Biblical Equality* offers well-crafted responses from a variety of scholars to a range of questions regarding the egalitarian theological position.[18]

---

[17]James R. Beck, ed., *Two Views on Women in Ministry*, Counterpoints (Zondervan Academic, 2005).

[18]Ronald W. Pierce, Cynthia Long Westfall, and Christa L. McKirland, eds., *Discovering Biblical Equality: Biblical, Theological, Cultural, and Practical Perspectives*, 3rd ed. (IVP Academic, 2021).

- *Gender Roles and the People of God* is a short but potent treatment of the egalitarian position, exploring the topic from theological, sociological, and historical perspectives.[19]
- *Rediscovering Scripture's Vision for Women* provides a deep dive into the contentious New Testament passages, laying out a compelling egalitarian interpretation for each.[20]
- CBEInternational.org is the internet home for the Christians for Biblical Equality organization. Its curated resources are searchable and numerous.[21]

Next, a number of thinkers have written generally about power and privilege over the last several years. Here are a few selected resources:

- *Subversive Witness*, referenced previously in this chapter, offers a compelling exhortation for Jesus-followers to leverage their privilege to overcome social inequality.[22]
- *Reckoning with Power* is a call to action for the church to use power in a way that benefits the common good.[23]
- *Tug of War* calls for a fresh look at power modeled after Jesus' journey with power and privilege, articulated so well in Philippians 2:1-11.[24]

Third, there is a small canon of books on allyship I have referenced here and there throughout *Allies in Ministry*. Each of these resources makes an appearance in this book:

---

[19]Alice Matthews, *Gender Roles and the People of God: Rethinking What We Were Taught About Men and Women in the Church* (Zondervan, 2017).

[20]Lucy Peppiatt, *Rediscovering Scripture's Vision for Women: Fresh Perspectives on Disputed Texts* (InterVarsity Press, 2019).

[21]CBE International, www.cbeinternational.org.

[22]Gilliard, *Subversive Witness.*

[23]David E. Fitch, *Reckoning with Power: Why the Church Fails When It's on the Wrong Side of Power* (Brazos, 2024).

[24]Wilmer Villacorta, *Tug of War: The Downward Ascent of Power* (Cascade Books, 2017).

- Among other things, *Better Allies* provides the framework for the seven distinct allyship roles surveyed in chapter four.[25]
- *Becoming an Ally* offers a deep dive on the roots of social oppression before engaging the topic of how to overcome oppression through allyship.[26]
- *How to Be an Ally* breaks down allyship into a seven-step process and functions as a how-to manual for would-be allies.[27]
- *Good Guys* is a must-read for anyone who is interested in continued reflection on the specific topic of male allyship. Authors David G. Smith and W. Brad Johnson are the experts on male allyship in the secular context, and their book is full of practical ideas for how to express allyship in the workplace.[28]

As they process their disruptive encounters with the notion of male privilege, one bit of good news for men is that they have sound resources to draw from. The resources above should provide an opportunity for men to synthesize their experience and hopefully remain on the allyship pathway heading into step four.

Further experiences. Like others referenced previously, Javier started out his allyship journey from an adversarial starting position. Because of this, when he noticed the women in leadership in his faith community ministering with obvious impact, he was propelled into a disruptive encounter with the notion of male privilege. For the first time in his life, he was witnessing God using the leadership of women to shape him as a disciple and a leader, and for Javier that required some serious pondering.

---

[25] Karen Catlin, *Better Allies: Everyday Actions to Create Inclusive, Engaging Workplaces* (Better Allies, 2019).

[26] Bishop, *Becoming an Ally.*

[27] Melinda Briana Epler, *How to Be an Ally: Actions You Can Take for a Stronger, Happier, Workplace* (McGraw Hill, 2022).

[28] David G. Smith and W. Brad Johnson, *Good Guys: How Men Can Be Better Allies for Women in the Workplace* (Harvard Business Review Press, 2020).

In response, Javier decided that he needed to investigate further, and he chose to place himself in even more contexts where women were leading. In effect, he was saying, "God has used these particular women in my life, but is this a normal thing in ministry? Could this in fact be God's intention for a woman's role in ministry?" To answer these questions, Javier intentionally sought out churches where women were preaching, committed to reading Christian books penned by women, and was careful to address his questions about faith and leadership to both the women and men in his life.

In the end, these choices to place himself under the leadership of women helped Javier to shift away from his adversarial starting position, moving along the continuum first to neutral and then to positive. Today, Javier is a strong ally to woman in his ministry context, and one thing that marks his allyship is his continued commitment to experiencing the leadership of godly women.

Like Javier, sometimes would-be male allies can benefit from further experiences that can help them interpret their disruptive encounter with the notion of male privilege. This choice to engage in more disruption can help men successfully journey through step three on the allyship pathway.

Process helpers. The Bible is clear that we need one another. In fact, the Bible commands us in Galatians 6:2 to "bear one another's burdens, and in this way you will fulfill the law of Christ." For men who are pondering their disruptive encounter with the notion of privilege, there is perhaps no greater resource than process helpers, people who can come along and help bear the burden of a man's disorienting dilemma. There are at least three categories of process helpers that can be useful in this context.

First, *pastoral* process helpers can help a man process his feelings of dissonance, helping him discern and interpret what Jesus is trying to say through his disruptive encounter with the notion of male privilege. "A spiritual guide is a godly, mature follower of Christ who shares knowledge, skills, and basic philosophy on what it means to increasingly realize Christlikeness in all areas of life."[29] This kind of pastoral guidance can be crucial for would-be male allies, especially for those with dramatic disruptive encounters.

Second, *mentors* can help men process their disruptive encounter by sharing aspects of their own journeys. This can be particularly useful because they can validate a man's experience in the dissonance; in effect, mentors are able to say, "You're okay; I've walked this road as well." As I will explore in detail in chapters seven and eight, habitual male allies, men who have traversed the pathway into step seven, can be excellent mentors at this point in the process.

Third, *coaching* process helpers are helpful in guiding people toward a response. "The coach's central thrust is to provide motivation and impart skills and application to meet a task or challenge."[30] Effective coaches can creatively discern next steps, and they can hold men who are pondering their disruptive encounter accountable to a legitimate process of discernment.

One final note on the process helper category of response bears mention, and that is the reality that both women and men can function in this capacity for men as they travel the pathway and respond well to their disruptive encounter with the notion of privilege. Several men interviewed for this project could point to women who walked alongside them as they processed their dissonant experiences early on this journey, and that is my testimony as well. That said, whether a woman should step in to help a man through this third step in the allyship pathway is a matter for

---

[29]Paul D. Stanley and J. Robert Clinton, *Connecting: The Mentoring Relationships You Need to Succeed in Life* (NavPress, 1992), 65. In their book, Stanley and Clinton break down the mentoring task into three categories: intensive, occasional, and passive mentoring. Each category has various role responsibilities assigned to it.

[30]Stanley and Clinton, *Connecting*, 73.

discernment; it is important that all parties feel comfortable with the arrangement.[31]

FINAL THOUGHTS

This chapter began with a story about Martin, a former student of mine who had a disruptive encounter with the notion of male privilege and ended up stepping off the allyship pathway. All these years later, this remains a sad story for me, because I just know that Martin could have become an effective ally to the women in whatever ministry context he found himself in.

It's tempting for me to despair whenever someone I'm investing in chooses to move away from the pathway. I know that it is not, but in many ways, it feels like a personal rejection. And so it has become important for me to remember that people can change. In the parlance of the sower parable, the soil might well be different the next time a would-be male ally experiences a disruptive encounter, and they may indeed opt to remain on the pathway.

Which brings me to Gary's story. Gary's early allyship biography was very similar to Martin's. Like Martin, he had been raised in a complementarian environment. Like Martin, Gary had experienced the dissonance of seeing women use their gifts with tremendous ministry impact. And like Martin, Gary had looked like he was on his way toward responding favorably and progressing on the allyship pathway. Unfortunately, also like Martin, after wrestling with the Scriptures, Gary opted to return to his starting position. As it was with Martin, it was hard for me

---

[31]One consideration could be around boundaries. In my book on flourishing mixed-gender ministry partnerships, I have a whole chapter exploring the concept of contextualized boundaries. In the chapter, I make that case that "women and men should thoughtfully discern what boundaries are right for their particular partnership in light of who each person is and is becoming and then live out those boundaries with integrity and accountability." The same principle would apply in the context of women functioning as process helpers to would-be male allies at step three. Rob Dixon, *Together in Ministry: Women and Men in Flourishing Partnerships* (IVP Academic, 2021), 128.

to watch Gary's allyship journey seemingly end before it really began.

So imagine my surprise some twenty years later when I got a message from Gary out of the blue. In his note, Gary let me know that he had had a change of heart and mind, and he now embraced an egalitarian reading of the Scriptures. He had read my book *Together in Ministry*, and he wanted to meet with me to talk about how the church he is pastoring could become a place that empowers women in greater measure. I was thrilled! Since that message, I've had the chance to do a bit of coaching as Gary has worked to bring change in his context.

Gary's story reminds us that people can change. Praise God that thorny, rocky, and impacted soil can be remedied. Even for men who initially opt off the allyship pathway, there is hope that one day they will find their way back to becoming the allies the church needs them to be.

QUESTIONS FOR REFLECTION

- What resources do you have available as you and/or the men in your life seek to process their disruptive encounters with the notion of male privilege?
- How might you go about gathering more resources? Which ones do you need?
- How can you cultivate a heart that is good soil, open to new ideas and experiences?

4

INITIAL ATTEMPTS AT ALLYSHIP

Several years ago, a college student named Troy came to our Women in the Bible seminar, the same seminar that was pivotal in Noel's journey from chapter two. For Troy and the other men in the seminar, the week served as a prolonged disruptive encounter, and my colleague Tammy and I had the joy of pastoring the students through their response to the experience. By the end of the week, they were ready to talk about action steps, and we encouraged Troy and the rest of the students to consider ways they could operate as allies to women in their ministry contexts.

Troy was a college football player, and as he contemplated our invitation to think through embracing an ally identity, he began to reflect on his experience on his team. In particular, he realized that his team's locker room culture was chronically disrespectful toward women, marked by sexist jokes and coarse language that was too often derogatory about women. As Troy put it, "The football locker room is not a place that honors women."

In response to our week together, Troy's commitment was to help change this locker room culture; to be specific, he pledged to call out his teammates when they made misogynistic, disparaging comments. I can't overstate how big of a deal this was for Troy to make this commitment, though I suppose it helped that he was at least six feet six inches tall and over three hundred pounds!

ALLYSHIP ROLES

At some point, having successfully responded to their disruptive encounter or encounters, would-be male allies take their initial allyship steps. They take their newfound conviction and begin to act on it. Those initial steps may be tentative, but they are almost certainly meaningful, as stepping out really kick-starts the process of shaping their identity as allies.

As I noted in the introduction, in her book *Better Allies*, Karin Catlin outlines seven different roles allies can play. In my research interviews, each of these roles made an appearance. Catlin's allyship activities range from quieter roles with little to no public risk to the ally to louder roles with a higher degree of public risk. Viewed on a continuum from quieter to louder, Catlin's allyship role rubric looks like figure 4.1.

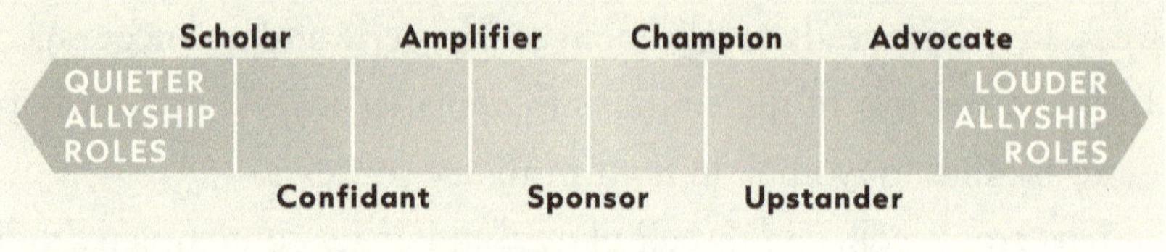

Figure 4.1. Catlin's allyship role continuum

In this chapter, I will begin by defining each of these seven allyship roles, going from quieter to louder varieties. Next, I will illustrate each role using a story in which Jesus operates as an ally to women. Finally, I will offer practical ideas and guidance for what it could look like for male allies to express these roles as they take their initial steps into allyship.

Scholar. The first part of our working definition of a male ally describes a man who is "engaged in an active process of understanding his privilege," and the scholar role dovetails well with that sentiment. When a male ally adopts a learner's posture and seeks to understand the experiences of women in his context as well as his own male privilege, he is operating as a scholar. Catlin defines a scholar as someone who "seeks to learn as much as possible about the challenges and prejudices faced by colleagues from marginalized groups."[1]

The challenge with talking about Jesus as a scholar is that he miraculously knows things about people.[2] Still, as a male ally, Jesus was intentional about asking questions as a way to enter into the world of women in his context. There are plenty of examples of this in the Gospels, but consider John 20:11-18, also referenced in chapter two. In the passage, the resurrected Jesus interacts with Mary Magdalene in a garden. It ends up being a crucial engagement, as Jesus shares the message of the resurrection with Mary and commissions her to tell the disciples, but the conversation starts with a thoughtful question from Jesus.

In John 20:15, Jesus wants to understand why Mary is weeping, and he also wants to know who she's looking for. Asking these questions puts Jesus into a learner's posture, and it also brings Mary's voice into the conversation. When would-be male allies operate as scholars, they emulate Jesus by putting themselves in a position to, in Catlin's words, "learn as much as possible" about the experiences of women in their contexts.

How can would-be male allies take on the role of the scholar? First, men can pursue a deeper understanding of the challenges women face in the church and in church ministry in particular by creating opportunities to listen and learn. In *Becoming an Ally*, Anne Bishop is a strong proponent of the scholar role, encouraging people with privilege to "learn everything you can about the oppression—read, ask questions, listen. Your ignorance is part of

---

[1]Karen Catlin, *Better Allies: Everyday Actions to Create Inclusive, Engaging Workplaces* (Better Allies, 2019), 24.

[2]We will examine the text in John 4 below in the context of the confidant role, but in that passage, Jesus demonstrates he already knows the truth about the woman's sexual/relational history, when, in John 4:17-18, he recounts the details of her story without her sharing them.

the oppression. Find people in the oppressed group who like to teach and see value in cultivating allies in general or you in particular. Ask them your questions."[3]

Books, articles, websites, podcasts, movies, and videos can all provide places to for would-be male allies to continue on their learning journey. For instance, in one survey response, a man mentioned that he faithfully listens to *Truth's Table* podcast as a way to better understand the realities Black women face as they navigate life in the church.[4] When men do the work to learn in these ways, it benefits them, but it can also be a blessing to women in their circles, who get a break from having to continually explain their lived realities, an experience that can be exhausting.

That said, a second thing that scholars can do is to invite women in their context to share their stories with them. Doing so will mean that male allies also take on the confidant role, discussed in detail below. One thing scholars will learn quickly is the importance of asking permission before entering into another person's world. As noted above, it can be exhausting for marginalized women to repeatedly share their experiences in an effort to educate others, so a simple question such as "Is it okay if I ask you about your experience?" would be a healthy way to enter such a conversation.[5]

---

[3]Anne Bishop, *Becoming an Ally: Breaking the Cycle of Oppression in People* (Fernwood, 2015), 97. Similarly, Melinda Epler lists learning as the first of her seven steps for taking action as an ally. Melinda Briana Epler, *How to Be an Ally: Actions You Can Take for a Stronger, Happier Workplace* (McGraw Hill, 2022), 41-70.

[4]*Truth's Table* (podcast), https://truthstable.com.

[5]Asking permission matters in part because not every member of an oppressed group will be in a place to take on a teaching role with would-be allies. As Bishop notes, "Do not expect every member of the oppressed group to be ready and willing to teach you. When you are in the ally role, you have privileges and comfort in your life that members of the oppressed group do not have because of the oppression; do not expect them to also give you their time and energy so that you can learn about them" (*Becoming an Ally*, 97). Because of this reality, would-be allies should take it slowly, learning at a pace that is comfortable for the women in their networks. In addition, they should also be intentional about learning from other sources, such as the ones referenced in chapter three.

Whether they learn from books and other content sources or from the women in their context, male allies who take on the scholar role focus on learning. There is a humble curiosity that is evident, and women in their circles can see and feel it. As would-be male allies make their initial attempts at allyship, the scholar role is often a good place to start.

Confidant. Generally speaking, confidants provide a context where someone from a marginalized community can let down their guard. Catlin notes that allies who operate as confidants "[create] a safe space for members of underrepresented groups to express their fears, frustrations, and needs. Simply listening to their stories and trusting that they're being fruitful creates a protective layer of support."[6] With this definition in mind, male allies operate as confidants when they provide a protected interpersonal environment for women in ministry.

As noted in chapter two, cultural norms dictated that Jesus was rarely alone with a woman, but that is the case in John 4:1-42. In the text, Jesus is in Samaria resting at a well when a woman comes to draw water. Jesus initiates a one-on-one conversation with this woman, a conversation that ranges from historic, cultural, and ethnic tensions to the woman's marital history, to ultimately Jesus' messianic identity. It is truly a remarkable interaction.

At least in part, this frank and significant exchange is made possible because Jesus is operating as a confidant. He begins the process of creating a safe space for this woman by immediately placing himself in a deferential position in John 4:7 when he asks her for a drink from the well. Next, by interacting with the woman in an honest and earnest way, Jesus cultivates an environment in which she can ask questions that ultimately result in her faith awakening, an awakening that then leads to her guiding her

[6]Catlin, *Better Allies*, 26.

community to a saving faith in Jesus. Because of her interaction with a true confidant, "in a powerful way, one that defies social convention, [this woman] carries out the functions of a true disciple."[7]

Male allies function as confidants to women in their context when they do several things. First, they prove themselves to be trustworthy stewarding private information. Instead of passing on things that are shared with them in confidence, they carefully and intentionally preserve secrets. In the case of male allies stewarding the personal experiences of potentially wounded women, discretion can be of paramount importance.

Second, confidants listen well. Reflecting on his experience as an ally, one male leader remarked, "I think the most important thing a male ally can do is listen carefully when women choose to share their experiences." Trusted male confidants deploy each of the hallmarks of effective listening, including eye contact, nonverbal engagement, and paraphrasing for understanding. Among other things, listening well builds trust, something confidants need in order to effectively function as allies.

Third, confidants know to give advice only after careful reflection. Simply put, confidants are slow to speak. Empathy makes an appearance in our working definition of male allyship, and the confidant role is one place where men can express empathy for women who have had to endure hardship. Indeed, sometimes the best thing a male confidant can give to a marginalized woman is validation, in the form of a simple phrase such as, "That's really hard."

Finally, sometimes the confidant role can be expressed in a more structured or formal arrangement. After discernment and with permission, men can be intentional about mentoring or coaching women, over time helping them prepare for greater leadership

---

[7]Kamila A. Blessing, "John," in *The IVP Women's Bible Commentary*, ed. Catherine Clark Kroeger and Mary J. Evans (InterVarsity Press, 2002), 599.

roles. In their book *Athena Rising*, W. Brad Johnson and David G. Smith write, "As a minority group in many organizations—always at risk of being marginalized—women encounter unique challenges and barriers to finding mentors, compared with their male counterparts. For this reason, intentional male mentors can be even more powerful and pivotal for women."[8] Purposeful mentoring is another way men can serve as confidants for women.

Amplifier. According to Catlin, amplifiers "[work] to ensure that marginalized voices are both heard and respected. This type of allyship can take many forms, but it is focused on representation within communication."[9] Male allies function as amplifiers when they choose to boost the voices and actions of women in the communication channels they have access to.[10]

When looking at the life and ministry of Jesus through the lens of male allyship, one thing that immediately stands out is how often women feature in the stories he tells as he teaches about faith. There are plenty of examples of Jesus operating as an amplifier for women in his storytelling, but perhaps none more vivid than Luke 21:1-4. In the passage, Jesus is with his disciples observing people making their offerings at the temple in Jerusalem. As Luke describes it, "[Jesus] looked up and saw rich people putting their gifts into the treasury; he also saw a poor widow put in two small copper coins. He said, 'Truly I tell you, this poor widow has put in more than all of them, for all of them have contributed out of their abundance, but she out of her poverty has put in all she had to live on.'"

What a powerful moment, one the disciples would likely have missed if Jesus hadn't chosen to amplify the actions of this woman.

---

[8] W. Brad Johnson and David Smith, *Athena Rising: How and Why Men Should Mentor Women* (Bibliomotion, 2016), 44.

[9] Catlin, *Better Allies*, 22.

[10] Amplifiers boost the voices of women; by contrast, sponsors and champions use their voices on behalf of women in their contexts.

By centering her actions, he presents her as an example of faith for his disciples to follow. Indeed, "in contrast to the scribes' pride and hypocrisy stands this woman who has sacrificed out of her life to honor God. So Jesus says, 'Beware of the scribes, but follow this widow.'"[11]

Would-be male allies can follow Jesus' example in amplifying the voices and examples of women, an activity that can take several forms. In my research interviews, respondents talked about how they have learned to be intentional about quoting women in sermons and, like Jesus, telling stories where women are the faith heroes. Others talked about making conscious choices to share posts from women on social media, choosing to listen to and then share podcasts by women, and recommending books written by women to their networks.

Each of these activities implies that would-be male allies are listening to the voices of women in the first place. Indeed, absent content that articulates the voices of women, there is nothing to amplify! Therefore, one place to start for would-be male allies is being intentional about diversifying the media they consume.[12]

Sponsor. Transitioning into some of the louder allyship activities, Catlin talks about allies as sponsors. She writes, "When an ally takes on the role of a sponsor, they vocally support the work of colleagues from underrepresented groups in all contexts, but specifically in situations that will help boost those colleagues'

---

[11]Darrell L. Bock, *Luke*, IVP New Testament Commentary Series (InterVarsity Press, 1994), 331. This widow's example becomes even more pronounced when juxtaposed with the passage immediately before it, Luke 20:45-47, where Jesus points out the hypocrisy of the scribes, a group of men who "like to walk around in long robes and who love respectful greetings in the marketplaces and the best seats in the synagogues and places of honor at banquets. They devour widows' houses and for the sake of appearance say long prayers. They will receive the greater condemnation" (Luke 20:46-47).

[12]This is where the scholar role, referenced above, comes in handy. A male ally who is choosing to learn about the experience of women will have plenty of fodder to use as an amplifier.

standings and reputations."[13] In the context of the pathway, would-be male allies take on a sponsor role when they leverage their voice to help women in their context advance in their leadership and influence.

Jesus was comfortable operating as a sponsor for women. One example comes from John 8:1-11, where a group of scribes and Pharisees seek to entrap Jesus by asking him to adjudicate the fate of a woman they have caught in the act of adultery. They drag this poor woman in front of Jesus and ask him what he thinks they should do to her.[14] In response, Jesus bends down and mysteriously writes in the sand, and then in John 8:7 he says to them, "Let anyone among you who is without sin be the first to throw a stone at her." His words indict these men, and one by one they slink away, ashamed. The passage ends with Jesus processing this experience with the woman, who leaves the encounter challenged to sin no longer and forgiven by Jesus.

Jesus' defense of this woman fits Catlin's definition of an ally as a sponsor. While scholars are unsure about what he was doing writing on the ground, what he says has the effect of leveling out the dynamics in the situation.[15] To be sure, the woman was a sinner, but so were the scribes and Pharisees. In this way, Jesus boosts this woman's standing; the men who exploited her brokenness in an effort to entrap Jesus are no better than she is. Indeed, "those who

---

[13]Catlin, *Better Allies*, 19.

[14]By this point in the narrative, Jesus is known for his works of compassion. For instance, in John 4–5, Jesus demonstrated his compassion by healing a number of individuals. Still, the law commanded (in Leviticus 20:10 and in Deuteronomy 22:22-24) the death penalty for people caught in adultery. These two values—compassion for people and fidelity to the law—frame the two sides of the trap the scribes and Pharisees were attempting to set for Jesus.

[15]Some scholars speculate that Jesus is listing the sins of the men who brought the woman to him. Others posit that Jesus is harking back to the words of Jeremiah 17:13, which talks about those who have forsaken God having their names written in the dust, as opposed to the book of life from Exodus 32:32 and Daniel 12:1. See Rodney A. Whitacre, *John*, IVP New Testament Commentary Series (InterVarsity Press, 1999), 207.

came to condemn ended up condemning themselves by not casting a stone."[16]

In an organizational setting, male allies adopt the sponsor role when they use their words to commend women to others. Recently, a male colleague of mine had the opportunity to recommend a woman for a higher-level position, and he used his voice to do so. Once the woman had taken the role, he went one step further and volunteered to tell the entire organization about her promotion.[17] By using his voice to encourage the organization to consider his female coworker, my colleague operated as a sponsor.

In their book *Good Guys*, Johnson and Smith talk about the importance of sponsorship, noting, "Sponsorship entails advocating for a woman—especially at key moments in her career—by creating visibility, supporting her promotions, and ensuring she gets the training and development opportunities she needs to soar."[18] Memorably, they go on to say that male sponsors should operate as "raving fans" for the women in their context. Indeed, raving fans make effective sponsors and effective male allies in general.

Champion. Champions are similar to sponsors, but according to Catlin, when an ally is operating as a champion they are functioning "in more public venues. Champions willingly defer to colleagues from underrepresented groups in meetings and in visible, industry-wide events and conferences, sending meaningful messages to large audiences."[19] The key with the champion role is its public-facing nature; a would-be male ally seeks to express his allyship with the widest possible public scope.

---

[16]Whitacre, *John*, 208.

[17]This second part of the story, the choice to share the news more publicly, is an example of the champion role, covered below.

[18]David G. Smith and W. Brad Johnson, *Good Guys: How Men Can Be Better Allies for Women in the Workplace* (Harvard Business Review Press, 2020), 153.

[19]Catlin, *Better Allies*, 20.

Jesus operated as a champion when he expressed allyship for women in crowded environments. In Mark 5:24-34, we see Jesus' identity as a champion on display. In the first verses of the passage, Mark is careful to tell us that Jesus was surrounded by people, that a "large crowd" had "pressed in on him." In that most public of settings, Jesus discerns that a faith-filled woman has touched his garment in her quest to be healed from twelve years of constant bleeding, something that would have rendered her ceremonially unclean and thus a social and religious pariah.

After she touches his garment, she experiences healing, and Jesus pauses and invites the woman to reveal herself. Once again, Mark reminds us of the public nature of this encounter, as in Mark 5:31, the disciples understandably cry out, "You see the crowd pressing in on you; how can you say, 'Who touched me?'" There, surrounded by a mass of humanity, Jesus champions her, commending her faith and publicly declaring her to be healed. The effect of Jesus' allyship action in this text would have been profound for this woman. No longer would she be an unclean outcast; now she would be restored to the community. In this text, "Jesus breaks social and religious custom to liberate a bound woman by restoring the wholeness of her body and consequently her social functioning."[20] Done in front of a large crowd, this is the work of a champion.

Male allies operate as champions when they take a public stand to highlight the contributions of women in their contexts. For instance, champions are intentional about giving credit where credit is due, and when a woman makes a vital contribution, they publicly acknowledge it as such. My friend Todd recently had an opportunity to champion a woman named Vicki in the context of his leadership team. Vicki was generally a quiet person on the team,

---

[20]Bonnie Bowman Thurston, "Mark," in Kroeger and Evans, *IVP Women's Bible Commentary*, 555.

not taking up much space. In one particular meeting, she opted to make a contribution that turned out to be especially insightful. After she'd spoken, Todd stopped the meeting, saying, "Did everyone hear that? Vicki just made a great suggestion." Because of his action as a champion, Todd's entire leadership team got to really engage this beneficial idea, and Vicki's voice was publicly affirmed and honored.

In addition, would-be champions choose to publicly make their convictions about gender equality known. In their research interviews, men talked about preaching sermons that highlight God's value for women, calling out injustice against women in public settings, and intentionally representing their value for women in leadership on public-facing websites and other promotional activities.

These examples capture the verbal aspect of operating as a champion, but it is also possible for male allies to champion women by their physical presence. For example, during his research interview, one man talked about his experience attending the women's rally that followed the presidential inauguration of Donald Trump in 2016. In his words, "It just felt important to me to stand in solidarity with women that felt threatened by a looming Trump presidency."

Alongside championing women using verbal and physical expressions, men can also opt to champion women on social media. What people retweet or post on Facebook and other social networks can influence their social circles, and would-be male allies think intentionally about what their social media presence communicates about their attempts at allyship. In this way, would-be male allies can combine the amplifier and champion roles to great effect.

Upstander. Upstanders step up and act in the face of injustice against a marginalized group. As Catlin notes, "When an ally takes on the role of the upstander, that ally acts as the opposite of a bystander. The upstander is someone who sees wrongdoing and acts to combat it. This person pushes back on offensive comments or jokes, even if no one within earshot might be offended or hurt."[21] Reflecting on the story that opened this chapter, Troy's commitment was to operate as an upstander with his teammates in that locker room.[22]

Without question, Jesus consistently took on the role of an upstander. Indeed, Jesus made it a habit of intervening when he encountered injustice or brokenness, and he did that with women in particular. The woman from Mark 5 is an example of this, as is the woman who anointed his body in Mark 14 and John 12. But for another example, consider Luke 7:11-17. In the passage, Jesus has just finished healing the slave of a Roman leader when he happens upon a funeral in progress. Luke sets the scene by describing the deceased as "his mother's only son, and she was a widow" (Luke 7:12).[23]

Evidently this mourning widow is present, and when Jesus sees her, he is "moved with compassion for her" (Luke 7:13).[24] At that moment, Jesus decides to become an upstander. Using his healing power, Jesus intervenes, and the man sits up and begins to speak before Jesus "gave him to his mother" (Luke 7:15). To be sure, most would-be male allies won't have the capacity to raise a man from the dead, but they should have the capacity to intervene when a woman is suffering or struggling in some way, provided their upstanding activity aligns with the stated needs of the women around them.

---

[21]Catlin, *Better Allies*, 25.

[22]Troy's allyship activity fits the upstander role the best, but there are also aspects of the champion and advocate roles in what he chose to do.

[23]As noted in the discussion about Naomi in the introduction, widows faced a particularly difficult road in first-century Palestine. Jesus' actions here would be a game changer for this particular widow.

[24]Once again, empathy is a key component of successful male allyship.

Taking on the upstander role implies a readiness to act, and that requires preparation. This preparation can take several forms. First, would-be upstanders can pray for eyes to see the injustice around them. Like Jesus in the Luke 7 text, would-be upstanders will want to be ready to engage the suffering of women whenever they encounter it, and one way for men to be ready is to ask God for sensitivity to observe the suffering of women in their contexts.

Second, upstanders mentally try on scenarios they might find themselves in. That is what Troy was doing at the end of that camp week. He was imagining what he might encounter the next time he was in the locker room and brainstorming how he might respond. In one interview, a male ally shared that he even creates scripts on his phone of things he might say should he come across some sort of injustice against women in his context, and that would be a beneficial practice for an upstander.

Finally, upstanders act when bystanders watch. In the crucial moment when a woman is being disparaged or treated unjustly, upstanders act.[25] "[Upstanding] can be the most difficult way to intervene, but often the most impactful, because you are recognizing and validating a person's experience when they are confronted by a microaggression, stopping it from continuing to create harm, and educating the microaggressor as well as any other people in the room."[26] All the preparation upstanders have done pays off as they open their mouths or move with their feet. And, Lord willing, the upstander's efforts result in bringing some level of healing and redemption in the midst of a painful situation.

---

[25]Smith and Johnson articulate something they call the "two-second rule." They write, "Within two seconds from the instant that sexist comment or demeaning joke rolls off a dude's tongue, say something" (Smith and Johnson, *Good Guys*, 113). Quick action is crucial for upstanders.

[26]Epler, *How to Be an Ally*, 143. Microaggressions are subtle but potent experiences that create marginalization.

Advocate. Advocacy is a powerful role for male allies to use. For some, *ally* and *advocate* function as synonyms, but it is important to realize that advocacy is just one way to express allyship. For Catlin, an advocate "uses their power and influence to bring peers from underrepresented groups into highly exclusive circles."[27] When male allies make choices to open up previously closed spaces on behalf of women, they are operating as advocates.

Jesus advocates for women in multiple stories in the Gospels, including Luke 10:38-42. In the text, Jesus and his disciples enter a village and stop at the home of Martha and Mary. As would be customary for a rabbi in those days, Jesus begins to teach, and Luke is careful to tell the reader in Luke 10:39 that it was Mary "who sat at Jesus's feet and listened to what he was saying."

This description is important because it positions Mary in a place women were typically not allowed. Indeed, the physical space at a rabbi's feet was reserved for men, this symbolizing the spiritually privileged position men enjoyed in the culture. As one commentator notes, "Serious disciples were preparing to be teachers—a role not permitted to women. Mary's posture and eagerness to absorb Jesus' teaching at the expense of a more traditional womanly role would have shocked most Jewish men."[28]

Ultimately, a challenge comes to Mary's choice to sit at Jesus' feet, and it comes from Mary's sister Martha. Rightly so, Martha wants to know why Mary is allowed to remain at Jesus' feet as opposed to fulfilling her culturally prescribed role in the kitchen. When Martha verbalizes her concern, Jesus takes on the role of an

---

[27]Catlin, *Better Allies*, 23. What differentiates the advocate role from the sponsor and champion roles is this final note about an ally endorsing women in "highly exclusive circles." The sponsor role majors on verbal affirmation in smaller, corporate settings; the champion role involves larger, more public contexts; and the advocate role focuses on exclusive settings where often the most power resides.

[28]Craig S. Keener, *The IVP Bible Background Commentary: New Testament* (InterVarsity Press, 1993), 218.

advocate, saying in Luke 10:41-42, "Martha, Martha, you are worried and distracted by many things, but few things are needed—indeed only one. Mary has chosen the better part, which will not be taken away from her." In Jesus' day, the space at the feet of a rabbi would certainly qualify as a "highly exclusive circle," and Jesus the advocate is more than happy to welcome women into that space.[29]

What could it look like to advocate for women as a male ally? First, it means noticing who is not in the room. Catlin writes, "The Advocate recognizes and addresses unjust omissions, holding their peers accountable for including colleagues of all genders, races and ethnicities, ages, body shapes, and sizes, religions, and sexual orientations."[30] In one interview, a man recalled a conversation about reproductive rights in which only men were in the room. Realizing this, he "paused the conversation and said, 'we should pick this up again when we can have women present.'" Male advocates have a lens that shows them when women are not in the room when they deserve to be.

Next, would-be advocates make attempts to open doors for women. In doing so, they put their voice and reputation on the line. In fact, sometimes advocating for access for women can bring a personal cost for men. They can be misunderstood, ridiculed, or worse.[31] But it is a cost they are willing to pay in the name of doing "intentional good" by opening up access to women.[32]

For easy reference, I have compiled these seven allyship roles into table 4.1.

---

[29]One argument for a complementarian understanding of the Scriptures is that Jesus selected twelve men to join his band of disciples. But as this text makes clear, Jesus was comfortable with women becoming his disciples as well.

[30]Catlin, *Better Allies*, 23.

[31]As noted in the following chapter, pushback is a reality that would-be allies can face as they live out any of these roles.

[32]Epler, *How to Be an Ally*, 119.

Table 4.1. Catlin's allyship roles with examples from the ministry of Jesus

Roles (from quieter to louder)	**Male Allyship Focus**	**Example of Jesus as a Male Ally**	**Practical Applications for Male Allies**
Scholar	Learning as much as possible about the challenges women face	John 20:11-18, where Jesus asks questions of Mary in the garden	Consume media produced by women and ask good questions in an effort to learn
Confidant	Creating safe space for women to share their experience and receive support	John 4:1-42, where Jesus creates safe space for the woman at the well	Listen well, protect private info, share only after listening, and provide support
Amplifier	Promoting the voices and examples of women using an ally's existing platform	Luke 21:1-4, where Jesus highlights the widow's sacrificial faithfulness	Profile the stories and voices of women in sermons, on social media, and in available networks
Sponsor	Vocally promoting women in an effort to boost their standing and reputation	John 8:1-11, where Jesus defends the woman caught in adultery	Function as "raving fans" for the women in their networks
Champion	Promoting women to larger audiences in whatever way possible	Mark 5:24-34, where Jesus publicly heals the bleeding woman	Promote women in public venues with the widest possible scope
Upstander	Intervening to stop injustice perpetuated against women	Luke 7:11-17, where Jesus steps in to heal the widow's son	With permission, be prepared to intervene if needed
Advocate	Leveraging privilege to bring women into exclusive spaces they wouldn't be able to access on their own	Luke 10:38-42, where Jesus defends Mary's choice to sit at his feet	Make attempts to open otherwise closed doors to women

FINAL THOUGHTS

The wonderful thing about Catlin's list of allyship roles is that would-be male allies have seven solid and diverse options to choose from. On the other hand, it can be overwhelming to have so many potential allyship roles. As male allies make their initial attempts at allyship, they will want to be discerning about which role(s) to inhabit in each particular situation. Choosing which allyship role to use in a given situation takes at least two questions into account.

First, how are would-be male allies wired? Some allies may be better equipped for the quieter allyship roles, and others for the louder ones. The best allies know how they are wired, and they operate out of that place more often than not, especially initially.

Second, what does the situation call for? Not all moments call for upstanders. Understanding the scenario is crucial for effective allyship, and when an ally's skill set overlaps with what the situation calls for, powerful things can happen. For more on the process of discerning which allyship role to use and when, see chapter six.

QUESTIONS FOR REFLECTION

- Have you ever been the beneficiary of any of these allyship roles? Which ones? How did it feel?
- Have you ever tried to take on one of these roles as an ally for others? Which ones? How did it go?
- As you consider how God has wired you, which of the seven roles seem like they would be a good fit for you?
- What tangible next step can you take to function as an ally in one of these areas in your ministry context?

5

PUSHBACK EXPERIENCE

When he got back from his meeting, Keith looked absolutely shell-shocked. In said meeting, he'd ventured onto step five on the male allyship pathway, the one marked by pushback, and he had all of the dissonant feelings you might expect.

As noted in chapter one, Keith certainly didn't start out as an ally to women in his ministry context. Instead, his journey began from an adversarial starting position. But over time, Keith had several disruptive encounters that challenged his view of the world. For one thing, he found himself involved in a ministry context in which women were actively using their gifts in every capacity. As he watched, he realized that his experience of seeing fruit from the ministry of these women didn't fit with the complementarian theological container he'd been given as a child.

That dissonance drove Keith to the Scriptures, and to his credit, he jumped into a theological discernment process wholeheartedly. At the time, Keith was training as a biochemist, and he approached the text as it if were an experiment to be carefully undertaken. He thoroughly examined the entirety of the Scriptures, with special attention given to the texts in the epistles that temporarily restrict the role of women in leadership. In the end, Keith's response to these two disruptive encounters was to embrace an egalitarian theology and practice, and he was eager to step out as a male ally in his ministry context.

One day, Keith found himself in a meeting of local ministry leaders. This collection of leaders was gathered for the purpose of working together to host a weeklong evangelistic outreach for college students. At one point in the proceedings, the group began to brainstorm a list of potential speakers for the centerpiece event of the outreach week, when someone would take the stage and invite students to put their faith in Jesus.

Perhaps unsurprisingly, when the brainstorming time was finished, every name on the whiteboard was a male name. Some men in room were on the list, as were other men from local networks. As he watched the conversation go in this direction, Keith resolved to put his newfound convictions into practice and to make his move as an ally. Adopting the advocate role, Keith summoned his courage and asked the group whether they could consider adding women to the potential speaking roster, and he proposed several local women who would be a good fit for the assignment.

Keith's proposal landed with a resounding thud. One of the men mumbled something about how this was a job for men, but no one else said anything. On top of that, no one made eye contact with Keith. Then, following an awkward silence, the meeting simply continued.

This experience was distressing and disorienting for Keith as a would-be ally. Later, as we processed what happened, I worried Keith might not respond well, that he might choose to opt out of the allyship pathway. So, it was a relief when he said, "You know what, I'd like to try again at our next meeting. Can you help me think that through?"

Days later, we met to strategize about what Keith might say during the group's next meeting. In the end, we created a flow chart to help him think through how the conversation might go.

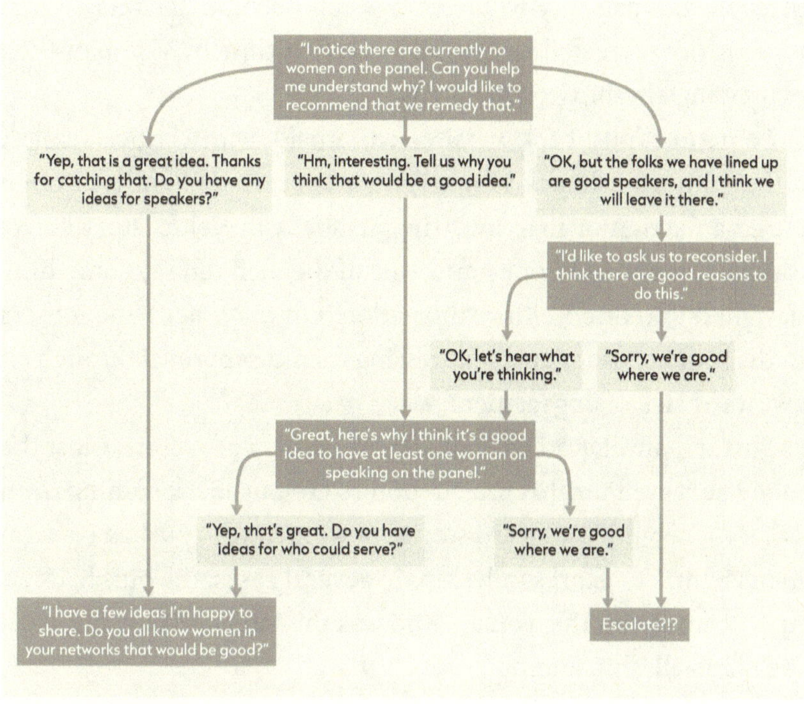

Figure 5.1. Advocating for women in leadership example flow chart

Unfortunately, this story does not have a happy ending, at least in terms of the ultimate decision. Keith's second attempt at advocacy was likewise rejected, and the group ended up never really considering a woman for the role. But for Keith, the process was the point. He had now weathered pushback because of his male allyship, and it galvanized him to continue on the pathway. As mentioned previously, today Keith is on the cusp of step seven in his male allyship.

THE REALITY OF PUSHBACK

The fifth step of the allyship pathway is marked by pushback. In this step, a would-be male ally makes an attempt—or, like Keith, multiple attempts—at expressing allyship, only to find others responding negatively to his efforts. For many men, this is the first place on the pathway where things can become personal, as critique is now directed at them for the first time by virtue of their expressing allyship in concrete ways.

Sometimes pushback is expressed verbally, with a critical remark. Other times pushback is nonverbal, expressed silently through either an action or inaction. The pushback in Keith's story above was a bit of both. On one hand, one of the men did say something designed to refute Keith's exhortation. On the other hand, others in the room chose silence, expressing their disapproval through an awkward lack of engagement.

Further, pushback can come from a variety of vectors. Most the men I surveyed for this project pointed to pushback coming from other men, but I also heard stories of women who pushed back on men's efforts to express allyship. In several cases, the pushback actually came from the woman who was the intended beneficiary of the man's allyship attempts.[1]

Whatever form it is delivered in and wherever it comes from, the experience of receiving critique can make it difficult for men to remain on the allyship pathway. In fact, this fifth step is the second place in the pathway where men might well opt out as they decide the pushback is just too much for them to bear, and they return to the allyship starting position.

PUSHBACK IN THE BIBLE

As would-be male allies navigate this fifth step in the allyship pathway, they will be encouraged to know that plenty of Bible characters experienced pushback as a result of expressing their convictions. While we do not get a glimpse of men in the Bible being critiqued specifically due to their allyship activities on behalf of women, it is clear that pushback comes with the territory when

[1]In one particular story, the woman was (rightly) concerned that her would-be male ally was centering himself in his allyship, a topic I will explore in more depth in chapter six.

people articulate what they see as a necessary truth in a given situation. Examples from Moses, Deborah, Paul, and Jesus will illustrate this point.

Moses has featured previously in this book, in chapter two in the context of the burning-bush passage from Exodus 3. That text represented the beginning of Moses' prophetic leadership journey, a journey marked by some serious high points, including the miraculous crossing the Red Sea and the delivery of the law on Mount Sinai. Unfortunately for Moses, his leadership journey was also marked by near constant pushback from those he was attempting to lead. Indeed, guiding the Israelites through the desert meant that Moses had to endure a steady stream of grumbling and complaining. Eventually, the pushback from his followers became so bad that Moses snapped, saying to God in Numbers 11:14-15: "I am not able to carry all this people alone, for they are too heavy for me. If this is the way you are going to treat me, put me to death at once—if I have found favor in your sight—and do not let me see my misery." It is quite a thing to be so bothered by pushback from your followers that you view death as preferable to having to continue to endure it!

Another Old Testament leader, Deborah, also faced pushback to her leadership. In Judges 4, we are given a window into her interaction with Barak, a military commander. In the passage, we learn that Deborah is judging Israel, meaning that she is "to be a savior, a guide, [and] a warrior for [God's people]."[2] As God's appointed judge, Deborah's words would carry maximum weight, and in Judges 4:6-7, we are told that she summoned Barak in order to give him the plan for the upcoming battle against their opposing army. Instead of simply receiving Deborah's command and then acting

[2]Ailish Ferguson Eves, "Judges," in *The IVP Women's Bible Commentary*, ed. Catherine Clark Kroeger and Mary J. Evans (InterVarsity Press, 2002), 132.

on it, Barak responds with doubt, letting Deborah know he will not follow her mandate unless she physically comes with him.

Deborah seems to interpret Barak's response as pushback to her leadership, because in Judges 4:9 she says, "I will surely go with you; nevertheless, the road on which you are going will not lead to your glory, for the Lord will sell Sisera into the hand of a woman."[3] Barak expressed his pushback in the form of doubting Deborah's leadership, and by extension God's choice to appoint Deborah as a judge, and there would be consequences for him.[4]

In the New Testament, the apostle Paul was also familiar with pushback, as he was famously opposed by plenty of people during his ministry career. In several cases, he even names his opponents in his letters. As just one example, consider 2 Timothy 4. In that chapter, Paul reveals that Demas, in love with the world, has forsaken him, Alexander the coppersmith did him great harm and strongly opposed Paul's message, and then no one showed up to his first defense. Given his relentless familiarity with pushback, it makes sense that earlier, in 2 Timothy 3:12, Paul writes, "Indeed, all who want to live a godly life in Christ Jesus will be persecuted."

Moses, Deborah, and Paul were plagued by pushback on account of their prophetic leadership, and of course Jesus was as well. As I mentioned in chapter three, Jesus was no stranger to criticism

---

[3]In the passage, the Israelites end up defeating their foe, and Deborah's prophetic gift is confirmed as the glory ends up going to a woman named Jael. After assassinating the enemy's leader in memorable fashion, Jael greets Barak in Judges 4:22, saying, "'Come, and I will show you the man whom you are seeking.' So he went into her tent, and there was Sisera lying dead, with the tent peg in his temple." In this way, "A defenseless, statusless, weaponless female becomes the victor over the erstwhile commander of 'nine hundred chariots of iron'" (Eves, "Judges," 133).

[4]It is worth noting that not all commentators see pushback in Barak's response to Deborah's leadership. Some view his request for her companionship as a reflection of his own self-doubt, and others speculate that he is simply eager for her wise counsel on the battlefield. Still, reading Barak's response as pushback is legitimate, given the significant negative consequences that result from his request.

and pushback from the religious leaders of his day; ultimately, Jesus' opponents were willing and able to condemn him to death.

As would-be male allies experience pushback at step five on the allyship pathway, they can be encouraged by two things. First, they can be reminded that they are in good company. Biblical leaders such as Moses, Deborah, Paul, and Jesus likewise endeavored to speak truth and then received pushback due to their convictions. Second, because Jesus in particular is familiar with pushback, would-be male allies have the perfect place to go to as they process their own experience. In fact, as was true with step three, each aspect of the pushback response cycle outlined below can be framed as an opportunity to interact with Jesus as men pursue a faithful response to their allyship pushback experience.

ALLYSHIP PUSHBACK RESPONSE CYCLE

Both from my research for this project and from my experience observing male allies in my ministry context, I have noticed a standardized cycle of response to pushback that comes as a result of a man's attempts to express his allyship. The cycle consists of six phases. The first phase is the allyship action step. This phase would include men taking on at least one of the allyship roles outlined in chapter four. The next phase is the pushback experience itself. Following that moment of pushback, would-be male allies then benefit from reflecting on four particular questions during the remaining phases. Engaging these questions can help men remain on the allyship pathway instead of taking the fork that leads back to the starting position. I will explore each question in greater measure in the sections that follow, but the four questions include:

- What is happening internally for men as they experience the pushback?

- What will men need in order to successfully process their pushback experience?
- Is there merit to the pushback, in terms of either presentation or the substance of a man's allyship activities?
- What is God saying to men through the pushback experience?

Visually, the allyship pushback response cycle looks like figure 5.2.

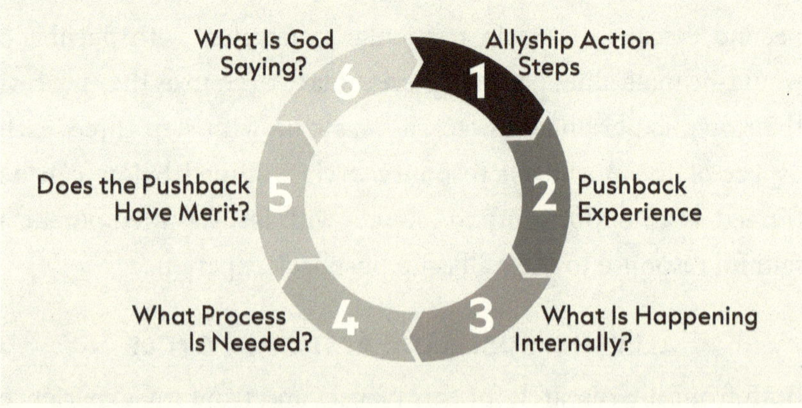

Figure 5.2. Allyship pushback response cycle

What is happening internally for men as they experience the pushback? In telling Keith's story at the very beginning of this chapter, I used the word *shell-shocked* to describe his immediate response following his initial attempt to express allyship. Many of the men interviewed for this study conveyed similar feelings. This third phase of the allyship pushback response cycle calls men to intentionally carve out space, even briefly, to sift the emotions they are feeling in response to the pushback.

In their book *Thanks for the Feedback*, Douglas Stone and Sheila Heen evocatively describe the emotional response that so often comes with receiving critical feedback. They write, "When we're in the grip of a triggered reaction we feel lousy, the world looks darker, and our usual communication skills slip just out of reach. We can't think, we can't learn, and so we defend, attack, or withdraw in defeat." Further, Stone and Heen articulate three specific triggers that hinder people from receiving feedback well. First, a truth trigger is set off when the substance of the feedback just is not accurate. Second, a relationship trigger is activated when the person delivering the feedback is in some way unpalatable. Third, identity triggers are about the receiver. "Whether the feedback is right or wrong, wise or witless, something about it has caused our identity—our sense of who we are—to come undone."[5]

As noted in chapter two, my wife, Amy, and I recently published a picture book titled *Penny Preaches*. As the title suggests, it is the story of a little girl who decides she wants to become a preacher. Even as we were writing *Penny*, we knew that there would be a sizable segment of the church that would object to even the premise that girls should aspire to grow up to become preachers.

It wasn't a surprise, then, when we started to get critique and pushback on social media, but it was still painful. A relatively prominent Christian leader, someone with a complementarian view of the role of women in ministry, got a hold of our publisher's announcement post and publicly lambasted our book as well as our publisher on social media. In response, anonymous posters piled on, and Amy and I found ourselves facing some harsh and painful words. In one particularly egregious post, someone wrote to us, "shut up, demons."[6]

I am someone who wants others to like me, and to say the least, getting labeled a "demon" doesn't comport well with that desire. To

---

[5]Douglas Stone and Sheila Heen, *Thanks for the Feedback: The Science and Art of Receiving Feedback Well* (Penguin Books, 2014), 15-17.

[6]Pastor Doug Bursch has written about how Christians might go about engaging well on social media, and he discusses the toxicity of internet trolling. He writes, "People who engage in trolling behavior frequently disregard the humanity of individuals who get in the way of their self-centered objectives. Trolling only has room for one person to be satisfied, one person to be considered, one person's ego to be fed." Being the target of internet trolls is not for the faint of heart. See Bursch, *Posting Peace: Why Social Media Divides Us and What We Can Do About It* (InterVarsity Press, 2021), 132-33.

borrow from Stone and Heen's typology, this was an identity trigger for me, and I certainly felt the temptations to "defend, attack, and withdraw in defeat." Thankfully, Amy and I managed to pause and talk through our emotions. Bringing trusted friends into that process was also useful for us.

Most of the time, when potential male allies hit pushback and subsequently opt off the allyship pathway, it is because an identity trigger has been ignited. A potential ally takes a stand, encounters a negative response, and in effect says, "I no longer want to identify as an ally in this situation. It's too hard." Faced with pushback, would-be male allies need to carve out space to really sit with how they are feeling, in part because it can guide their response. That is the focus in this third phase of the allyship pushback response cycle.

What will men need in order to successfully process their experience? In his research interview, one man told a story about a time he had used the upstander allyship role to call out a sexist joke that one of his male friends had told when they were golfing. In response, the other two members of the group attacked this man, accusing him of being "oversensitive" and a "buzzkill." W. Brad Johnson and David G. Smith have a term for this experience: the wimp penalty. The wimp penalty is the "fear of being penalized for speaking up on behalf of someone leads to concerns about negative perceptions and . . . backlash."[7] In this case, the wimp penalty was in effect, and with a rueful shake of his head, this man told me that their unpleasant interaction "made the next few holes pretty awkward." He was rattled, troubled, and confused.

By its very nature, pushback can hurt. In fact, pushback can function like the disruptive encounters discussed in chapter two. Because of this, many of the response categories articulated in chapter three are useful here in phase five as well. Once they have clarity

[7]David G. Smith and W. Brad Johnson, *Good Guys: How Men Can Be Better Allies for Women in the Workplace* (Harvard Business Review Press, 2020), 21.

about what they are feeling in response to their pushback experience, would-be male allies can engage the question about which resources they will need in order to effectively process their experience.

For instance, community can help would-be male allies successfully navigate this pushback step. In his survey response, one man recounted the following story:

> I once served as a local church pastor, and there were a number of occasions on which I would invite a female pastor to come and preach for me when I would be out of town. Always, before each these services, I would receive a comment, email, or note from certain parishioners letting me know that they would not be attending that week because I was having a woman come speak. Their response bothered me every time.

In order to process this pushback, this man noted, "I went to my denomination, which was affirming of women in leadership, and I was able to get guidance from mentors for how to engage people on this topic. I also used denominational curriculum to try to educate my congregation." This man's story illustrates the importance of having community support as men express their allyship.[8]

Community support can be a useful tool as men process allyship pushback, but the other processing mechanisms from chapter three will be helpful as well, including space to process, journaling, prayer, focused Scripture study, further reading, and more. Making the determination about which avenues to use in processing pushback is the primary focus of this fourth phase of the pushback cycle.

Does the pushback have merit? A third question to engage on the allyship pushback response cycle is the question of merit. As a

---

[8]This story also illustrates the importance of organizational support. When would-be male allies know they have the power of their organization behind them, they may be willing to be bolder in their allyship activities.

would-be male ally processes his pushback experience, it is important to discern whether there is something in the pushback worth receiving as a useful corrective. In other words, is the pushback deserved because of how the male ally chose to express his allyship?

Sometimes the way would-be male allies express their allyship is in some way off-putting. Perhaps in their zeal to express their initial attempts at allyship, would-be allies browbeat others or come off as in some way condescending. To be sure, often allyship calls for men to be direct and even forceful, but if allies begin to belittle others, then they have crossed a line. Pushback related to tone can help men understand where that line is, and they can then learn how to stop short of it in future allyship efforts.

Other times, pushback may reveal that something is unhelpful or incomplete in the substance or content of a would-be ally's presentation. In this way, pushback can also provide useful feedback that can make future allyship attempts more effective.

For the last few years, my friend Karl has been faithfully functioning as an ally on his church's leadership team, encouraging the all-male group to consider rethinking its complementarian theological position on women in leadership. Not long ago, Karl was able to secure time in the team's agenda for a presentation on egalitarian theology, and he invited me to come provide the content. I jumped at this allyship opportunity, and because it is so often the theological epicenter regarding this topic, I opted to focus my presentation on 1 Timothy 2. I offered what I thought was a careful and nuanced reading of the text from an egalitarian perspective.

Because of its prominence in this theological conversation, I have done a lot of work with that text over the last decade or more. But I was still underprepared for the fusillade of questions this group of men asked me. They wanted to parse just about every word of the passage, and I found myself saying, "I don't know the answer to that" probably six or seven different times. My presentation was simply not up to the task. The experience with those men caused me to redouble my efforts to understand that particular text, including embarking on a deeper exploration of both the context of the passage and the Greek words Paul employs in his writing. Ultimately, my hope is the pushback I received during that experience will make me a more effective presenter the next time I am given such an opportunity.

As would-be male allies receive pushback, they should make space to consider it carefully. Perhaps there is in fact something that they could have done differently. A humble learning posture is crucial as men respond to pushback in phase five of the allyship pushback cycle.

What is God saying through this pushback experience? The allyship pushback response cycle culminates with space for men to focus on discerning what God is saying to them through the pushback experience. Male allyship is certainly a technical enterprise; in other words, it is truly a skill set that can be developed. But it is also a spiritual endeavor, and this sixth phase of the cycle centers that reality. At this point in the allyship pushback response cycle, men have identified and processed their emotions around receiving pushback, and they have sought to humbly learn from the experience. Now is the time to listen to what God wants to say to them though the experience. I recommend four categories of reflection topics at this phase in the cycle.

First, what is God saying to men about who they are as a disciple? It could be that the pushback experience reveals a defect in a man's character that might require attention. Or perhaps there is something about a man's character that has emerged that is commendable and therefore worthy of focused development. God is always working in our lives to shape us at a character level, and it is crucial for men to consider how they are being formed as a disciple in the midst of an allyship pushback experience.

Second, what is God saying to men about the people who provided the pushback? We live in a polarized environment in which we are too often encouraged to vilify those who disagree with us on important matters. It is crucial to understand that this malevolent posture toward people who push back at us runs counter to how Jesus would have us respond to others. Consider Jesus' words from the Sermon on the Mount in Matthew 5:39-40: "If anyone strikes you on the right cheek, turn the other also, and if anyone wants to sue you and take your shirt, give your coat as well." This radical statement is meant to "shock the imagination and instill a profounder insight into God's intention. The old ways of retaliation and self-protection must give way to a gentler, more magnanimous approach to those we deem enemies."[9] Even as would-be male allies hit a relationship trigger and are really hurt by a person who wielded their critical feedback like a club, they are instructed to treat that person with dignity and respect.

Third, what is God saying to men about their future on the allyship pathway? Again, step five is the second place on the pathway where men might choose to move away from continuing to develop as an ally, but for men who aspire to continue onward, it is vital to understand what God is saying to them in the midst of the pushback. For instance, like Keith, many interviewees talked about how the experience of weathering pushback galvanized them in their allyship identity. In this way, these men were able to turn the step-five pain and dissonance into conviction. After time and space to process the experience with the Lord, the pushback

---

[9]Douglas R. A. Hare, *Matthew*, Interpretation: A Bible Commentary for Teaching and Preaching (John Knox, 1993), 58.

experience actually ended up functioning as an accelerant for their allyship journeys.

Finally, what would God have men do next? With this question, the cycle returns back to where it began, as would-be allies answer the question about tangible next steps. For some men, God might invite them to reengage and try again. That was Keith's sense of his faithful next step. For other men, the best next step might actually be to disengage and wait patiently for another allyship opportunity further down the road. This is where discernment comes in, and discernment is not one size fits all. Male allies should be judicious about next steps, following their best sense of what God might call them to do.

Once again, pushback is hard. It can trigger us and cause real pain, so we must thoughtfully process it. My hope is that breaking down the response process into these six phases will help would-be allies synthesize their pushback experience, thus empowering them to remain on the allyship pathway.

FINAL THOUGHTS

As I write this chapter, I am sitting with this question: Can you be an ally if you haven't experienced personal pushback because of your allyship? I think the answer is no. There's truly no way around this fifth step in the pathway, and if a would-be male ally has not experienced some form of pushback because of their allyship attempts, they may need to consider whether they are doing enough to express their allyship convictions.

Pushback is not fun for would-be male allies, but it is survivable, and it can even become a clarifying and empowering experience for men. This was the apostle Paul's experience. In 2 Corinthians 11:16-33, Paul articulates a list of his sufferings, many of which involved pushback from others, even including violent physical punishment. In the text, Paul notes he has been imprisoned, flogged countless times, lashed on five different occasions, beaten by rods three times, stoned once, and in danger from a wide range of factions. Ultimately, these experiences served to propel Paul's work; indeed, he views these various forms of pushback as badges of honor, writing in 2 Corinthians 11:30, "If I must boast, I will boast of the things that show my weakness." Pushback is embedded in the allyship journey; the only question is, How will men respond to it?

QUESTIONS FOR REFLECTION

- Generally speaking, how are you at dealing with criticism? Where are your growth edges in responding to pushback?
- Have you ever experienced pushback due to your attempts to express allyship in some context? What happened? How did you feel?
- How does the allyship pushback response cycle help you as you think about successfully navigating step five on the allyship pathway?

6

CONTINUED INVESTMENT

NOT LONG AGO, I got the chance to do some consulting work with a church whose stated goal was ordaining women into leadership. It is difficult to fully capture just how comprehensive this change process was for the church and its congregants. This church had traditionally been hostile to women's leadership, both in the pulpit and in the pastoral office. Becoming a church that ordained women would require a holistic change approach, including theological, structural, cultural, and interpersonal considerations, among others.

It was an honor for me to function as a consultant for this church's pastoral leadership team, and slowly but surely we worked through the various issues. The team started by reconsidering its bylaws, opening the door for women's leadership at a policy level. Next, the pastors focused on intentionally developing women who could become viable candidates for ordination. On top of these things, the church courageously waded into often fraught theological waters, crafting safe spaces for congregants to explore egalitarian theology and consider its ramifications for ministry in the church.[1]

---

[1]Around this time, a colleague and I did some research and were able to outline a template process for how churches might go about shifting their theology from complementarian to egalitarian positions. See April Fiet and Rob Dixon, "Making the Shift: A Roadmap for Churches Moving to Full Inclusion of Women in Church Leadership," Missio Alliance, 2021, https://missioallianc1.wpenginepowered.com/wp-content/uploads/2021/10/Making-the-Shift_Missio-Alliance-Article.pdf.

After several years of process, the day finally arrived as a gifted woman named Elaine was ordained into leadership. I got a chance to watch a recording of the ordination service, and it was certainly a joy-filled occasion. Many months of careful work had gone into making that day a reality, and the sense of satisfaction was palpable, even through the video screen.

Not long after the ordination service, I had a conference call with Elaine and her male copastors. They confirmed the experience I'd had as I had watched the video, testifying about how much fun it was to celebrate what God had done. Then one of men exclaimed, "After the journey we've been on as a congregation, it feels so rewarding to be here at the finish line."

Unfortunately, this pastor's phrasing struck me as all wrong, and I decided to risk spoiling the jubilant moment to offer what seemed to me to be needed perspective. I said, "I think you need to see this achievement not as the finish line, but as the starting line. Now is the time to really roll up your sleeves and get to work courageously living out your convictions."

It can be tempting for male allies who successfully navigate step five to take their proverbial foot off the gas. Indeed, after progressing through the initial five steps, it may feel to men as if they have actually arrived as newly minted allies. But like the church mentioned above, in many ways step six represents a secondary starting line on the allyship pathway. Even though they have come a long way, would-be male allies continue to have developmental work to do.

ONGOING ALLYSHIP INVESTMENT

Step six on the pathway is labeled the continued investment step. In this step, men have begun to see themselves as allies, and they are motivated to go deeper in their ally experience. It is as if steps one through five represent Allyship 101, and in step six, would-be male allies enroll in a 201-level experience.

Interestingly, this pivot often brings with it a sense of excitement and even zeal. In the continued-investment step, male allies tend to feel like they are now engaged at a personal level. My friend Wayne is a good example. Starting in the predisposed positive starting position, Wayne moved quickly through the first four steps on the pathway. Pushback came in the form of the wimp penalty when Wayne was mocked by men from his home group because of his egalitarian convictions.[2] Emerging from that experience, Wayne became an ardent ally for women in his church community. For instance, he began to look for opportunities to challenge his complementarian friends, often in what he labeled "aggressive ways."[3]

The challenge for men like Wayne is tempering their zeal and retaining their learner's posture, understanding that they continue to have room to grow as allies. And for more-seasoned mentors who journey with men through the pushback response cycle, it is important to remind their protégés they will need to continue to invest in their development as allies in step six.

THE BIBLICAL THEME OF INVESTMENT

Investment is a theme in the Bible. Jesus' parable in Matthew 25:14-30 points to the importance of a person understanding what they have been given and then investing it in order to maximize its impact. In the passage, Jesus tells the story of a man who is going

---

[2]As noted in chapter five, the "wimp penalty," a term coined by Smith and Johnson, occurs when would-be male allies get negatively critiqued from others as a result of their attempts at allyship. David G. Smith and W. Brad Johnson, *Good Guys: How Men Can Be Better Allies for Women in the Workplace* (Harvard Business Review Press, 2020).

[3]I pressed him for an example of what he meant by "aggressive ways," and Wayne mentioned that following his pushback experience, he began to create theological debates within his peer group. By his own admission, some of those debates were not healthy ones, as they were motivated from his personal place of pain.

away on what turns out to be a long trip. Before he goes, this man gives money to three servants. One servant is given five talents, a second is given two, and a third is given just one.[4]

When he finally returns from his journey, the man gathers his servants and demands an accounting. The first and second servants come forward and report they have doubled their money by investing it well. In response, the man lauds their efforts, saying in Matthew 25:21, 23, "Well done, good and trustworthy slave; you have been trustworthy in a few things; I will put you in charge of many things; enter into the joy of your master."

In contrast, the third servant presents the same single talent he was given at the beginning of the story. Instead of investing it and doubling it like the other servants, this servant had buried it in the ground, afraid of losing it and thus receiving punishment from his master. This result angers the master, and he pronounces a penalty on the third servant, saying in Matthew 25:27-30,

> You ought to have invested my money with the bankers, and on my return I would have received what was my own with interest. So take the talent from him, and give it to the one with the ten talents. For to all those who have, more will be given, and they will have an abundance, but from those who have nothing, even what they have will be taken away. As for this worthless slave, throw him into the outer darkness, where there will be weeping and gnashing of teeth.

To be sure, this is a challenging teaching, but it speaks to the importance of followers of Jesus investing what they have been given with the hope of greater impact. More to the point, the message of the parable is that people need to invest what they have or they

---

[4]"Although the exact value of a talent varied from period to period and place to place, we may estimate the values of these investments at roughly fifty thousand, twenty thousand and ten thousand denarii. Since one denarius was a day's wage, this would be a 'small sum' only to a very rich master, who would probably entrust his wealth only to his most dependable and prudent servants." Craig Keener, *The IVP Bible Background Commentary: New Testament* (InterVarsity Press, 1993), 117.

could well lose it entirely. In the words of one commentator, "Whereas the other servants are rewarded by the master's benevolence, this servant, fearing the master's harshness but unaware of his benevolence, experiences the very wrath he feared. This, says Jesus, is what will happen to those who claim to be his followers but do not invest their lives in the work of the kingdom."[5] For Christians in general and for male allies in particular, the message is to take what we've been given and invest it for greater impact.

CONTINUED INVESTMENT IN THE CONTEXT OF THE ALLYSHIP PATHWAY

After would-be male allies navigate the pushback experience in step five, the invitation for them is to take what they have experienced so far on the allyship pathway and to invest it by going deeper. Allies at this step in the pathway don't rest on their laurels. Instead, they strive to hone their allyship skills, taking risks and stepping out of their comfort zones. My research suggests that there are five main areas of focus for men in this continued-investment step: further reflection on the notion of male privilege, diversified allyship roles, greater discernment with allyship skills, increasing comfort with not being at the center, and sharing the allyship journey with others.

Further reflection on the notion of male privilege. One focus for men in the continued-investment step relates to their male privilege. In step six, men deepen their reflection on the reality that that world tilts in their favor as men, a journey that began back in the disruptive-encounter experience of step two. In chapter two I introduced the idea of men becoming a "privilege detective," in the context of an exploration type of disruptive encounter. As men transform into privilege detectives, they develop lenses to see male privilege around

[5]Craig S. Keener, *Matthew*, IVP New Testament Commentary Series (InterVarsity Press, 1997), 359.

them in their ministry contexts. The privilege detective idea is largely an *intra*personal one; that is, it is mostly about a male ally growing in self-awareness about the privilege he benefits from.

In step six, male allies add an *inter*personal facet to their reflection on the notion of privilege. I've coined the term "privilege prophets" to describe a male ally's responsibility to challenge others to consider the reality of male privilege. Privilege prophets intentionally call out privilege in others, leveraging the upstander role to help others become aware of situations in which privilege is in play. In operating as a privilege prophet, step-six allies might well find themselves creating a disruptive encounter for a less-seasoned male ally.

I recently had a chance to be a privilege prophet. I was conducting a training with a cohort of women who were training to be preachers, and at the end of my presentation, the women were invited to ask questions from their ministry contexts. One woman mentioned that her church's leadership team had declined her request for a churchwide theological discernment process, at least in part on the grounds that the topic of women in leadership is a "secondary issue."

I discussed the issues with labeling the topic of women in leadership a secondary issue in chapter one in the context of a neutral starting position. Here I will add that this label often seems to be applied from a place of privilege. That is, sometimes men in power can dismiss the conversation because it doesn't affect them or their leadership. In essence, male privilege can shield men from engaging in this conversation in the first place. A male colleague of mine learned this lesson the hard way when he chose to bring a charged theological conversation about women in leadership to an abrupt end on the grounds that it was not a salvific issue. In reply, one of the women present retorted, "This topic impacts my life and calling every single day!" At that moment, my colleague realized he had made that statement from a place of his male privilege.

After I explained all of this on the video call, several of the women said that they had never thought of the "secondary issue" framing in that way, and they were grateful for this new way of interpreting comments like that one. As they progress into step six on the allyship pathway, men would be well-served to invest in their allyship by continuing to explore the notion of male privilege, and one way to do that is to become a privilege prophet in addition to continuing to function as a privilege detective.

Diversified allyship roles. The continued-investment step also includes an expanded use of the various allyship roles. In particular, male allies in this step might begin to try out roles that are initially unnatural or even threatening for them. For instance, allies who might prefer a quieter mode of expression might take steps to be a bit louder in their allyship, and vice versa.

That was my experience as I navigated step six. My nature is to prefer the more behind-the-scenes types of allyship roles, and that was especially true when I was further down the allyship pathway. For example, I was comfortable filling the scholar and confidant roles as I journeyed through step four. If I am being honest, the prospect of being more verbal or public about my allyship and using the upstander and advocate roles terrified me.

After I successfully weathered the pushback step, I was buoyed by the same zeal Wayne experienced. As a result, I was open to trying out several of the other allyship skills. At one point, an opportunity came when I received an invitation to represent Jesus' views on the role of women in leadership in the context of a panel discussion that included people from a wide range of perspectives on the topic.

I took the assignment seriously. I spent hours shoring up my understanding of the passages we would be discussing. I was meticulous in my preparation, writing out my answers to the panel questions word for word. As the event approached, I engaged my supervisor and other ministry partners, asking them for input on my planning document. I also asked just about everyone I knew to pray for me. And then I committed to myself that I would be brave during the panel discussion, speaking truth even if other panelists had dramatically different perspectives.

The day came and I did my presentation. It was not easy, but it was successful. In the end, the experience constituted an important investment in my development as an ally. I learned a lot through the process of creating and then executing the event. For instance, I gleaned a lot of new perspectives on the various disputed Bible passages. I also learned the value of relying on my community to help me though my angst. Most importantly, I discovered that I could indeed be more public in my allyship, a lesson that continues to propel me to this day.

Continued investment can mean pursuing bolder and more vigorous allyship roles. Or, if male allies are naturally predisposed to the louder allyship roles, it can mean embracing the quieter ones. Either way, not content to only use the allyship roles they are comfortable with, male allies expand their portfolio during step six on the allyship pathway.

Greater discernment with allyship skills. Alongside a more vigorous use of allyship roles, including unfamiliar ones, allies in step six become practiced at discerning the right allyship roles to use at the right times. Just as it doesn't make sense to use a hammer on a project that calls for a wrench, it could be unhelpful or even harmful to use the advocate allyship role in a scenario where the scholar role is needed.

By his own admission, Luis is a hard charger. He's a man of action, describing himself as someone who "shoots first and asks questions later." Unsurprisingly, Luis gravitates toward the louder allyship roles. He's naturally disposed to adopting the champion, upstander, and advocate roles. Ruefully, in his research interview, he told me a story about a time when his hard-charging temperament got in the way of his allyship.

Paula, a female colleague, was experiencing consistent marginalization in their team meetings. The main problem was that she would make suggestions that would routinely be ignored by her predominantly male colleagues. At one point, Paula approached her male team leader to share about her experience and voice her concern. In response, he made promises about keeping an eye out for her, but nothing had changed. In a place of frustration and pain, Paula brought Luis into her discomfort. Luis was outraged. He hadn't observed the dynamics Paula was describing on his own, but he was offended on her behalf. Luis's wife was a pastor, and he self-identified as an ally to women.

At a subsequent team meeting, Luis noticed Paula getting ignored, and without thinking he blurted out, "Why are we ignoring Paula's input?" Within seconds, Luis's question had blown up the meeting. People asked Luis what he was talking about, and he tried to offer examples but only ended up confusing the group. The leader was offended, as were several of the other men Luis had clumsily named. Most importantly, Paula was mortified as she had to watch her experience exposited publicly, out of her control.

Luis used the wrong allyship role in that meeting. He used the upstander role, breaking in to disrupt a situation where a woman was being marginalized. Sadly, the more appropriate role would have been the confidant role. His colleague needed his private support, not his half-cocked public intervention. Luis had taken matters into his own hands, and as a result he had caused more damage in the situation.

How might male allies go about discerning which role is the best one to use in a particular situation? The following three questions can help.

First, which roles are a man's preferred options? As noted previously, especially early on in the allyship journey, men will probably have a bias toward one or more roles. Most likely, like Luis, their preferred roles will align with their temperament. Before picking an allyship role to use, would-be male allies need to be aware of their default settings. Are they stepping into that particular role only because it suits them? Increased awareness will help men not just utilize the roles they are comfortable with.

Second, what is really happening in the situation? Paying close attention to the scenario can provide the data needed in discerning the proper allyship role to employ. One issue in Luis's story is that he was unaware of the problem his female colleague was articulating. He simply wasn't paying attention and looking for adverse gender dynamics on their team.[6] The nature of the situation should help answer the question of which role is appropriate, so would-be male allies should be careful observers and students of what is happening.

Third, how would a man's female colleague like them to be involved, if at all? If he had it to do over again, Luis would have used the confidant role, listening to Paula share her pain and then asking her whether or how he could support her as an ally. Ultimately, would-be male allies must defer to the women they are seeking to support regarding what form allyship should take. In fact, one of the dangers for would-be male allies is depriving or usurping a woman of her agency in their zeal to be an ally, which is what happened in Luis's story.

---

[6]In *Together in Ministry*, I coined the term "adverse gender dynamics" to refer to under-the-surface yet potent forces that tend to marginalize women in organizational or communal settings. By their very nature, adverse gender dynamics are "subtle and sneaky, and they take willful work to identify." In my book, I exhort organizations and individuals to be on the lookout for adverse gender dynamics, because if they can see such dynamics, they can mitigate them. Rob Dixon, *Together in Ministry: Women and Men in Flourishing Partnerships* (InterVarsity Press, 2021), 109.

It will take time and experience for male allies to learn how to deploy the allyship roles in the right situations. In fact, even the most-seasoned allies will occasionally make a mistake. Only continued investment will help men become more proficient at discerning the proper use of the available allyship roles.

Increasing comfort with not being at the center. Several years ago, I was presenting on my doctoral research at a gathering of leaders from Christian nonprofits from around the world. It's not uncommon for my presentations to be challenging for men to receive, since I talk about topics such as men laying down power, doing their inner work, and being careful not to marginalize women, either by their actions or lack of action.

At this event one man caught my attention, primarily because I watched him slowly but surely disengage over the course of my presentation. Early on, he was very involved with the content, asking insightful follow-up questions, responding both to my questions and those from his small group, and even laughing at the appropriate times. But as the session went on, I noticed that he got quieter, he stopped making eye contact, and increasingly when I looked up, he was scrolling on his phone.

At the end of the training day, we broke into groups to process the day, and I made sure to join his group. When it was his turn to share about his experience, he said something that has stuck with me. Specifically, he talked about how disorienting the day was for him, that "if the goal is become a church where men and women share power in this way, I don't know where my place is as a man."[7]

This man is not alone. Most men I interact with are used to being at the center of whatever process or conversation is happening

[7]My experience with this man provided the impetus for me to start thinking about male allyship as a topic. As I processed this man's experience in the seminar, I found myself asking, "What hopeful, generative vision can I give a man in this place?" Embracing the identity of an ally is one way to answer this question.

around them, and that is especially true in ministry settings. To return to Catlin's analogy referenced in the introduction, many men are more than comfortable being the knights in shining armor. That is the reality of male privilege, that by and large a given system caters to men. So it can be uncomfortable for men to move toward the margins, which is often where male allies operate, joyfully ceding the spotlight to the women they seek to empower.

The good news for men who might be experiencing dissonance in no longer automatically being in the center is that Jesus made a similar move to the margins. In chapter three, I referenced Philippians 2:1-11 in the context of responding well to a disruptive encounter with the notion of male privilege, and it is worth returning to that passage here. In everlasting communion with the Father and Spirit, Jesus was located at the very center of divine power but ultimately gave that up in order to empower humanity via the incarnation. So as male allies move further toward the margins, they follow the way of Jesus. Hopefully, that knowledge will aid in their spiritual formation as male allies.

Expressing allyship from the margins is not easy. That is why this sixth step on the allyship pathway tends to bring with it a formation component, as men are invited to find fulfillment and contentment while not being in the center.[8]

Sharing the allyship journey with others. On this sixth step on the allyship pathway, developing allies tend to become more vocal about sharing their experiences with others. In particular, they may start to share about their allyship experiences with other men

[8]Sometimes men's allyship attempts carry them into the center. Smith and Johnson have a term for this dynamic as well: the "pedestal effect." When the pedestal effect is in play, "men are given special treatment and shout outs for even small acts of gender equality." This is "understandably grating for women who for years have done the emotional labor and carried the load for equality with nary a man in sight." W. Brad Johnson and David G. Smith, "How Men Can Become Better Allies to Women," *Harvard Business Review*, October 12, 2018, https://hbr.org/2018/10/how-men-can-become-better-allies-to-women.

in their networks. And as this happens, they might begin to influence those men to embark on their own allyship journeys. In this way, step-six allies begin to function as allyship evangelists.

My colleague Peter's allyship has proved to be contagious, but it didn't start out that way. Ever since he arrived at step four, Peter has been a consistent and faithful ally to the women in his ministry context, but he has always been super quiet about it. This quieter brand of allyship suits Peter's temperament; unlike Luis from above, being the center of attention doesn't come naturally to Peter.

My sense is that Peter will always be first and foremost a quieter kind of male ally. Still, as he has grown in his allyship, Peter has started to share his journey with other men. For example, Peter has been intentional about telling allyship stories with the men he is mentoring, thus encouraging these less-seasoned men to consider beginning their own allyship journeys.

As men begin to share their allyship journeys with other men in their networks, they would be well-served to be up front about three things. First, allyship takes development. At this book attests, becoming an ally is not a one-time thing; instead, a whole pathway of development lies ahead of would-be male allies. Second, the allyship road can be a tough one. If men are going to embark on the allyship pathway, they deserve to know they will at points be confronted by their own failures, and they will almost certainly experience pushback because of their allyship. Finally, there is joy in the allyship journey, as male allies get to be a part of women in their context thriving and becoming the leaders God has called them to be.

Ministry leaders will say that often the best evangelists are the newly converted, primarily because they have a passion for faith that is evident and unquenchable. Similarly, men who are actively progressing on the allyship pathway are the best advertisements for male allyship. And the good news is that as men share their allyship journeys with other men in their networks, they are simultaneously investing in their own allyship development.

FINAL THOUGHTS

Considering the parable of the talents from Matthew 25 leads to focusing primarily on the actions of the third servant. This emphasis is good and right because disciples of Jesus need to understand what not to do when it comes to the choice of whether to invest our assets in the ongoing work of God's kingdom.

That said, we ought not to forget the other side of the story. Indeed, we need to note the good news in Jesus' story—namely, that for the two servants who opted to actively put their talents to work, they managed to double their investment. On top of that, as the text notes, upon his return, the master promised them greater leadership responsibilities along with what must have been a compelling and surprising invitation to "enter into the joy of [their] master."

In many ways, step six on the allyship pathway represents a second starting line for would-be male allies. And in the same way that the investment choices of the first two servants bore dividends, male allies should expect likewise expect benefits, including greater personal satisfaction in their allyship work and more effective support for the women in their ministry contexts.

QUESTIONS FOR REFLECTION

- If you are a male ally, how might you be tempted to think you've arrived after navigating the pushback step? How does this chapter challenge you to see step six as a second starting line?
- This chapter articulates five areas of continued investment for would-be male allies. Which ones challenge you as you think about where you need to grow as an ally?
- What are your practical next steps? How specifically will you invest in your male allyship in step six?

7

HABITUAL ALLYSHIP

I WAS EXCITED TO SIT DOWN with Lamar to hear about his journey on the allyship pathway, since I consider him a quintessential male ally. I have watched him operate in ministry for more than thirty years, and I know that Lamar is someone who has consistently and diligently invested in the women in his context. Indeed, dozens, if not hundreds, of women have been helped by Lamar's able use of each of the allyship roles described in chapter four.

Because of this, I was initially surprised when Lamar balked at using the label *ally* to describe himself. When I asked him about other words that he might be comfortable with, he demurred before finally saying, "Look, this is just who I am and how I operate." Lamar's answer stood out to me because he made the process of supporting women in his ministry setting sound so natural, so organic. Simply put, Lamar has made allyship a habit.

HABITUAL ALLYSHIP DEFINED

In this seventh and final step on the pathway, men arrive in the place of habitual allyship. Like Lamar, they have come to embrace the values and practices of an ally, and the concrete allyship roles flow naturally and fluently out of who they are. In fact, several male allies I interviewed for this book used the language of *identity* as they described how they think about themselves as allies. For instance, one interviewee said, "Being an ally to women is a core part of who I am at an identity level. And it's a part of my calling in ministry." The notion of an allyship identity struck me as an important concept.

Over the years, plenty of writers have focused on the importance of identity in the context of the Christian life. To be sure, a person's identity in Christ is a multifaceted concept, but three aspects of identity and identity development are germane to men's embracing an allyship identity at step seven on the pathway.

First, a person's identity formation is a process. People aren't fully formed right away; instead, identity formation takes time and comes as a person matures in their faith. Author and pastor Peter Scazzero describes the identify formation process this way:

> Living and swimming in the river of God's deep love for us in Christ is at the very heart of true spirituality. Soaking in this love enables us to surrender to God's will, especially when it seems so contrary to what we can see, feel, or figure out ourselves. This experiential knowing of God's love and acceptance provides the only sure foundation for loving and accepting our true selves. Only the love of God in Christ is capable of bearing the weight of our true identity. God has shaped and crafted us internally—with a unique personality, thoughts, dreams, temperament, feelings, talents, gifts, and desires. [God] has planted "true seeds of self" inside of us. They make up the authentic "us." We are also deeply loved. We are a treasure.[1]

This reality, that identity formation is a process that involves soaking and knowing, dovetails nicely with the whole concept of the allyship pathway. Identity formation, like ally formation, is a process. So we should expect that men won't fully identify as allies until they have progressed through each of the seven steps;

[1]Peter Scazzero, *Emotionally Healthy Spirituality* (Thomas Nelson, 2006), 75.

becoming an effective male ally to women in ministry is a journey, not a one-off experience.

Second, we all have a God-given identity, and it is crucial that each Christian seeks to discern what that is. Alongside other spiritual formation thinkers including Scazzero, psychologist David Benner uses the term "true self" as a synonym for a person's God-given identity, writing,

> There is, however, a way of being for each of us that is as natural and deeply congruent as the life of the tulip. Beneath the roles and masks lies a possibility of a self that is unique as a snowflake. It is an originality that has existed since God first loved us into existence. Our true self-in-Christ is the only self that will support authenticity. It and it alone provides an identity that is eternal.[2]

Perhaps not every man will end up holding his allyship at an identity level like this, but the pathway can and does provide a context for discerning whether male allyship is indeed a part of a man's true self. In particular, processing a disruptive encounter and weathering pushback will provide a platform for discerning a man's allyship identity. Gaining clarity on that will help men embrace allyship as who they are instead of merely something they do.

Third, a clear and established sense of identity should power a person's vocation. Benner puts it this way:

> God's will for us is that we live out the harmonious expression of our gifts, temperament, passions and vocation in truthful dependence on God. Nothing less than this is worthy of being called our

---

[2]David G. Benner, *The Gift of Being Yourself: The Sacred Call to Self-Discovery* (InterVarsity Press, 2004), 15. Of course the opposite of the true self is the false self, the identity that gets formed not by God but by us. Reflecting on a confrontation with his false self, M. Robert Mulholland Jr. writes, "I began to realize that underneath the thin veneer of my religiosity lived a pervasive and deeply entrenched self-referenced being which was driven by its own agendas, its own desires, its own purposes, and that no amount of superficial tinkering with the religious façade made any appreciable difference." Mulholland, *The Deeper Journey: The Spirituality of Discovering Your True Self* (InterVarsity Press, 2006), 23.

> true self. Nothing less than this will lead to our deepest fulfillment. And nothing less than this will allow us to show the face of Christ to the world that we have been called from eternity to show.[3]

A man's allyship will be more effective if it is tied to his sense of identity, as it will both bolster him when allyship is hard and fuel him to function as an ally over the long haul.[4]

As they explore and deepen their allyship identities at this final step of the pathway, male allies are primarily focused on two specific things. First, they continue to hone and perfect their allyship skills, seeking to become experts at their craft. Second, they intentionally invest in less-seasoned allies who are further down the pathway.

HONING ALLYSHIP SKILLS

Continuing with one of the investment emphases from step six, habitual allies seek to more fully develop in their use of the allyship roles described in chapter four. Even though allyship will come more naturally at this point on the pathway, habitual allies know that there will always be room for improvement. In particular, there are two places for habitual allies to focus as they seek to hone their craft.

First, habitual male allies will continue to develop competence with each of the allyship roles. At this point on the pathway, allies have moved beyond inhabiting only the roles that feel more natural to them, and they are able to use each of the roles with competence

---

[3]Benner, *The Gift of Being Yourself*, 103-4.

[4]This brief survey has majored on Christian thinkers and writers, but identity and identity formation are also areas of emphasis for secular psychologists. Indeed, corporate America has come to realize the importance of identity in the workplace. As one consultant notes, "In my work coaching and advising senior leaders, I have been obsessed with figuring out what separates average performance from extraordinary performance. It turns out that identity plays a critical role. Consider the very best performers in athletics and the arts. Virtually every one of 'the greats' identified as great before they had evidence that they were indeed extraordinary. In fact, they were absolutely convinced and certain of their greatness. It was their entire identity." Darren Gold, "The Power of Identity," Forbes, May 21, 2019, www.forbes.com/councils/forbescoachescouncil/2019/05/21/the-power-of-identity/.

if not excellence. Lamar, the habitual ally referenced above, is someone who has become fluent with each of the allyship roles. During our interview, Lamar told stories about using each one of the allyship roles, and that intrigued me. By his nature, I know Lamar to be wired for the louder allyship roles, and he certainly did share stories about how he has sponsored and advocated for women in public settings. He's also willing to use the upstander role if needed. And yet he also referenced the quieter allyship roles. For instance, Lamar operates as a scholar by reading new books that come out about the dynamics of women and men working together in ministry.[5] Habitual allies have an ever-developing knowledge of all seven allyship roles and have a basic competence with each.

Second, men at step seven are becoming more intuitive about which allyship roles are the right ones to use in a given situation. This idea of discerning the right role at the right time made an appearance in chapter six as one way allies invest in their development. By step seven, it's a much quicker process. By virtue of experience and their accrued wisdom, habitual allies can make the correct call about role discernment in shorter order.

MENTORING EMERGING MALE ALLIES

A second focus for habitual allies is seeking out less-developed men to shepherd as they progress on their own allyship journeys.

---

[5]It might be tempting to think men will be either a louder ally or a quieter one, but it's really a false dichotomy. Lamar's journey illustrates this well. He is clearly a hard charger and is more than willing to engage as an ally in public spaces. But he is also very much a scholar. Lamar began his pathway adventure from an adversarial starting position but was hired to serve in an egalitarian context. Not long after he was hired, his supervisor caught wind of Lamar's complementarian theological leaning and pulled him aside, saying, "You won't last long banging that headship drum around here." That conversation constituted Lamar's disruptive encounter, and he responded by entering a period of intensive study. He read books from both sides of the argument, and he made space for his own theological reflection, eventually emerging as a committed egalitarian. Lamar's inclination as a scholar on this topic has marked his entire pathway experience, and it is a wonderful complement to his more vociferous allyship activities.

In this way, these step-seven allies become mentors for those who come behind them on the pathway. Mentoring has been a bit of a theme throughout this book, making appearances in the context of disruptive encounters in chapter two, responding to disruptive encounters in chapter three, and helping men process their pushback experiences in chapter five. So it is no surprise that mentoring is a key function for habitual allies here at step seven.

According to leadership development theorists Paul Stanley and Bobby Clinton, "Mentoring is a relational experience in which a mentor, who knows or has experienced something, transfers that something (resources of wisdom, information, experience, confidence, insight, relationships, status, etc.) to a mentoree, at an appropriate time and manner, so that it facilitates development or empowerment."[6] In one sense, mentoring is a fundamentally human endeavor. "Spiritual mentors are not gurus or advice dispensers or answer people to every situation or question, but rather they are ordinary people who offer a wise presence that shows interest in us by asking questions and listening, by discerning and praying with us."[7]

On the other hand, there is something sacred about the mentoring role; it is also a spiritual endeavor. Certainly, the Bible has a category for the importance of mentoring. Writing to his own mentee Timothy, the apostle Paul says in 2 Timothy 2:1-2, "You then, my child, be strong in the grace that is in Christ Jesus, and what you have heard from me through many witnesses entrust to faithful people who will be able to teach others as well." "Timothy,

---

[6]Paul D. Stanley and J. Robert Clinton, *Connecting: The Mentoring Relationships You Need to Succeed in Life* (NavPress, 1992), 40. In their book, Stanley and Clinton group seven mentoring roles into three categories. Intensive mentoring configurations include disciplers, spiritual guides, and coaches. Occasional mentors include counselors, teachers, and sponsors. And passive mentors include contemporary and historical models.

[7]Randy D. Reese and Robert Loane, *Deep Mentoring: Guiding Others on Their Leadership Journey* (InterVarsity Press, 2012), 188.

like every other minister and every other believer, is a link in the chain of redemption. Each believer has received the gospel as a stewardship. And it carries the obligation to pass it on similarly to others."[8] Indeed, Paul's words to Timothy provide us with a holy strategy for developing others: namely, from one mentor to the next to the next. In the context of the male-allyship pathway, habitual allies can offer this mentoring help in one-on-one settings as well as in the context of a smaller group of men.

Individualized mentoring. For Lamar, individualized mentoring of less-seasoned men is built into his job description. Mentoring younger leaders is just a part of his ministry role. That said, Lamar has latitude about the topics he chooses to bring up with the men under his care. When I asked him where the topic of male allyship fits on his priority list, he said, "Every man I raise up, I want them to be an advocate for women." Simply put, if a man is being mentored by Lamar, he will be exhorted to become a male ally sooner or later.

Along with Lamar, habitual allies can choose to invest in less-seasoned allies, guiding them along the allyship pathway. The sections below contain a grid for how to select mentees as well as guidelines for fruitful mentoring relationships.

Group mentoring. Individualized mentoring is an effective way for habitual allies to raise up the next generation of allies, but mentoring can be a more communal experience as well. Several years ago, I created an opportunity to invest in less-seasoned men in the context of a group mentoring cohort. First, I obtained permission from my female supervisor and other prominent women in our community to gather a group of up-and-coming male leaders in our ministry into what I called a male allyship cohort. Before we

---

[8]Philip H. Towner, *1–2 Timothy & Titus*, IVP New Testament Commentary Series (InterVarsity Press, 1994), 170.

launched, I designed a syllabus of sorts and recruited candidates to join me for a nine-month journey through the allyship pathway.

I had four hopes for this cohort. First, I wanted to see each individual man grow as an ally, trying out tangible action steps during his time in the cohort. Next, I built theological reflection into the program, with the intention of solidifying and deepening each man's existing egalitarian theological convictions. Third, I fully intended to leverage the communal context for peer support and mentoring; I longed for our group to become a robust learning community. And finally, I built a project into the curriculum; toward the end of their time in the cohort, each cohort member was to host an egalitarian theological seminar for the faith communities they were leading.

Our cohort met monthly, and before each meeting cohort members were asked to read two books recommended in chapter three. Specifically, they read Smith and Johnson's book *Good Guys: How Men Can Be Better Allies for Women in the Workplace*, to surface tangible ally behaviors, and Peppiatt's book *Rediscovering Scripture's Vision for Women: Fresh Perspectives on Disputed Texts*, to shore up their egalitarian theology. When we were together on Zoom, we would discuss the readings and then discern application steps for the coming month. The hope each month was to take a risk and try out at least one of the allyship roles and then report back to the group at the following meeting. To help with the risk-taking aspect of the program, cohort members were paired off each month for accountability and support.

The entire cohort experience was a joy! We both celebrated our wins and consoled, supported, and challenged one another, and the cohort context allowed us to form a community that seemed to accelerate the pathway journey. Further, to my great satisfaction, the theological seminars were a gift to the faith communities these men were a part of, even functioning as disruptive encounters for male students who were able to attend. But perhaps even more significantly, those seminars were a gift to the men of the cohort, offering opportunities to use each of the allyship roles discussed in chapter four.

We ended the cohort on a public note as I heralded the completion of the cohort on our faith community's primary communication channel. The response from our community was fantastic, and together we celebrated this collection of developing allies on a Zoom call.

To be sure, individual men can journey the allyship pathway on their own, but transformation is often hastened in a communal setting. Jesus was aware of this reality; after all, he decided to gather a community of disciples as his primary mode of influence, as opposed to meeting only with individuals.[9] As faith communities invest in guiding men through this pathway, I encourage them to consider taking a cohort-based approach.

DISCERNING WHOM TO INVEST IN

As habitual male allies seek to mentor their less-seasoned brothers, either individually or in groups, it will help to be thoughtful in their selection process. Habitual allies should consider the following five considerations when picking men to invest in.

First, habitual allies should look for men who regularly work alongside women in their ministry context. In other words, it is important that mentees have a ministry context in which they can exercise allyship. In fact, if potential mentees do not have a viable context in which to live out their allyship convictions, would-be mentors might want to hold off until they do.

---

[9]Often, when Jesus would meet with individuals, that meeting functioned as a gateway into a discipleship community. For instance, Peter has a transformative one-on-one meeting with Jesus in the first part of Luke 5:1-11, but, by the end of the passage, "they" are leaving everything and following Jesus.

Second, mentors need to discern whether a potential mentee is of a sufficient level of personal maturity to make him a safe person for women to work with in the ministry context. In my doctoral research, I identified "awareness of gender brokenness" as one of ten attributes of flourishing mixed-gender ministry partnerships. "By way of definition, 'gender brokenness' refers to areas of struggle in our lives that stem from our experience as women or men."[10] For men, that would include things such as pornography consumption, objectifying women, and unconscious gender biases. As habitual male allies go about selecting men to mentor, they must interrogate where those men are regarding their gender brokenness, and gaining input from the women in their context could be a helpful as well. It is imperative that would-be male allies are safe for the women they are aiming to support. First, do no harm.

Third, teachability is crucial. Thinking back to the parable of the soils, would-be mentors will want to find less-seasoned men who have a fourth soil posture to new things. This is particularly true if those men might have impediments to seeing their male privilege and ultimately embracing the identity of a male ally. As noted in chapter one, men who are on the adversarial end of the allyship starting position continuum will have a lot to overcome if they are to progress along the allyship pathway, so teachability is key.

To be sure, it can be difficult to discern someone's level of teachability, but there can be outward signs that indicate an inner fourth soil posture. Writing on the *Lead Bravely* blog, pastor and leadership coach Kevin Lloyd points to five external metrics: Teachable people talk about what they are learning, take notes when they are in a position to learn something new, limit distractions when they are in a learning environment, choose to lean into learning opportunities, and are friends with people in their field who know

---

[10]Rob Dixon, *Together in Ministry: Women and Men in Flourishing Partnerships* (IVP Academic, 2021), 53.

more than they do.[11] There may be other ways to determine teachability, but these five external attributes are a great place to start.

Fourth, in 2 Timothy 2:1-2, which I referenced above, Paul specifically tells Timothy to look for faithful people to mentor. In context, the word Paul is using here connotes reliability or trustworthiness. In addition to being teachable, then, would-be mentees need to also be faithful, meaning they take the allyship development process seriously and are intentional about progressing along the allyship pathway. Habitual allies will want mentees who follow through on commitments to process disruptive encounters, try out allyship activities, endure through pushback, and pursue continued investment. As with teachability, a person's level of faithfulness can be difficult to gauge, but if a man has demonstrated faithfulness in other areas of his life as a disciple, he could be a good fit for mentoring in the context of the allyship pathway as well.

Fifth, habitual allies should look for men who will be able to pass on what they have learned to others. Again 2 Timothy 1 is instructive, as Paul specifically tasks Timothy with choosing individuals who can pass on the gospel to other faithful people. It is worth noting that this was Jesus' methodology as well.

> Jesus intended for the disciples to produce his likeness in and through the church being gathered out of the world. Thus his ministry in the Spirit would be duplicated many-fold by his ministry in the lives of the disciples. Through them and others like them it would continue to expand in an ever-enlarging circumference until the multitudes might know in a similar way the opportunity which they had known with the Master.[12]

As habitual allies choose their mentees, they should look for a capacity for multiplication. Men who are influential in their networks

---

[11]Kevin Lloyd, "5 Ways It's Visible That Someone Is Teachable," *Lead Bravely*, June 8, 2016, www.leadbravely.org/blog/2016/6/8/5-ways-its-visible-that-someone-is-teachable.

[12]Robert E. Coleman, *The Master Plan of Evangelism*, 30th anniversary ed. (Revell, 1993), 97.

and naturally gain followers would be good candidates for this kind of mentoring investment.

PRACTICAL MENTORING CONSIDERATIONS

What does this kind of mentoring look like in practice? Stanley and Clinton offer what they call the "10 Commandments of Mentoring," and this set of best practices can help habitual allies effectively mentor up-and-coming male allies in their ministry contexts.

First, at its core, mentoring is about relationship. As Stanley and Clinton note, "The stronger the relationship, the greater the empowerment."[13] Habitual allies should aim for a continually developing relationship, one marked by honesty and care. Further, since relationships and trust develop over time, allies at step seven should take on would-be allies to mentor only if each party has adequate time to invest in growing the relationship.

Second, clarity of purpose is important in mentoring relationships. Stanley and Clinton state, "Expectations should be expressed, negotiated, and agreed upon at the beginning of a mentoring relationship. . . . Along with expectations, [people] need to discuss and mutually affirm the purpose or basic aims of the mentoring relationship."[14] With the male allyship cohort, I clarified our purpose and goals first in the syllabus and then during our initial meeting. Then we returned to those core statements in our final meeting, using them as a way to assess what God had done during our nine months together. Both mentors and mentees will benefit from clarity about what the mentoring relationship is about and what would constitute a successful experience together.

Third, Stanley and Clinton advocate for some level of regularity in interactions. For mentoring relationships to succeed, there must be consistent time together. Earlier I noted that the cohort met

---

[13]Stanley and Clinton, *Connecting*, 198.

[14]Stanley and Clinton, *Connecting*, 198.

monthly, but I have also hosted other cohorts that met weekly. The same goes with individual mentoring relationships. I have also mentored less-seasoned male allies in shorter bursts, such as a three-session scenario. Whatever the frequency of interaction, regular connection is key.

Fourth, healthy mentoring partnerships have clarity about accountability. In a mentoring context, a mentor often gives tasks to the mentee. An up-front conversation about accountability dictates what will happen if those tasks are not fulfilled.[15] For example, a mentoring meeting might need to be postponed if the mentee fails to complete the assigned allyship task.

Fifth, Stanley and Clinton call for building healthy communication mechanisms, primarily so that there is clarity about how a mentor might speak truth to their mentee. The question Stanley and Clinton propose a mentor asking is, "If I see or learn of an area of need or concern for you—and it may be negative—how and when do you want me to communicate it to you?"[16] Asking and answering a question such as this one not only clarifies the communication process, but it also establishes the reality that hard conversations might well come with the mentoring territory. As I have walked men through their allyship journeys, I can think of plenty of conversations in which I have opted to address a growth edge, including faulty theological thinking, inaccurate views of self, and poorly executed allyship activities.

Sixth, mentors and mentees would be served by having a conversation about confidentiality. Specifically, what are the expectations about confidentiality in terms of what is shared in the mentoring context? By and large, the allyship mentoring

[15]As noted above, faithfulness is something to look for as habitual allies set up mentoring relationships with would-be male allies. Ideally, faithful mentees will not need much in the way of accountability.

[16]Stanley and Clinton, *Connecting*, 203.

relationships I have been a part of have operated with the assumption that everything discussed is confidential unless specified otherwise, but clarity around this is beneficial. Particularly as would-be allies process their disruptive encounter during step three and respond to pushback during step five, having a safe and confidential space to share is vital.

Seventh, healthy mentoring relationships have established checkpoints at which mentors and mentees evaluate how long the mentoring relationship should keep going. It may be that habitual allies will walk less-seasoned allies through the entire pathway, but it is also possible that the mentoring arrangement will last only for a step or two. Stanley and Clinton issue the following instructions: "Set realistic time limits. Have exit points where both parties can leave without bad relations. Have open doors where the invitation to continue can be open. [And] recognize the necessity of a time limit in any mentoring situation."[17]

Eighth, mentors should build evaluation moments into the rhythm of the mentoring relationship. Our cohort evaluated our experience at the end of its life cycle, but we could have done evaluative check-ins more often than that. As habitual allies go about their influencing work, it is wise to have a frank conversation about how the partnership is going, one in which expectations are revisited and any existing relational tension gets processed.

Ninth, Stanley and Clinton encourage mentors and mentees to modify expectations if needed. It makes sense to potentially readjust expectations following a robust evaluative discussion. It may be that the frequency of mentoring meetings needs to change in some way, or perhaps the confidentiality agreements need to shift. Fruitful mentoring arrangements are ever evolving, and this ninth commandment reflects that.

---

[17]Stanley and Clinton, *Connecting*, 205.

Tenth, habitual allies and their mentees should be intentional as together they bring the mentoring relationship to an end. Stanley and Clinton write, "A happy ending for a mentoring experience involves closure, in which both parties evaluate, recognize how and where empowerment has occurred, and mutually end the mentoring relationship."[18] In the particular context of a habitual ally and their mentee closing off a mentoring relationship, it seems right to revisit the mentee's pathway progression and to celebrate the change that has happened over time.

Alongside continuing to hone their allyship craft, habitual allies are proactive about investing in the next generation of allies. Following these ten mentoring principles should assist habitual allies in helping less-seasoned allies along the pathway in greater measure.

FINAL THOUGHTS

I will share one more Lamar story to close this chapter. During our video interview, when I was asking him whether he had anything else he wanted to say on the topic of male allyship, Lamar suddenly remembered an upcoming meeting he had with a woman he was supervising. He quickly pulled up his agenda for the meeting, which is something he sends to his supervisees ahead of their times together, and he read me one of his agenda items: "Do you ever pick up patriarchy from me?"

What a question to ask! At first, I couldn't believe he would be that blunt. Wouldn't that question put his supervisee in an awkward position? If she answers the question in the affirmative, what happens next? Wouldn't a positive response cause pain or put a strain on their working partnership? And was Lamar really willing to be critiqued in that way?

---

[18]Stanley and Clinton, *Connecting*, 207-8.

That's when it hit me: Habitual allies such as Lamar carry their allyship with humility. Because they have come to see themselves as allies at an identity level, they are open to correction, knowing that input from people around them will make them more effective in their allyship.

QUESTIONS FOR REFLECTION

- Do you know men who have fully adopted the identity of a male ally? How can you tell allyship is a habit for them?
- What could it look like to continue to hone your craft with the allyship roles? Which ones need more development in your life, and what could it look like to become proficient with them?
- For step-seven allies, what could it look like to invest in less-developed male allies in your community? Whom could you invest in? What are your faithful next steps?

8

A CALL TO ACTION

My friend and colleague Tim is one of my favorite male allies. Tim is a habitual ally, and he carries his allyship with a compelling balance of earnestness and gentleness. Tim's allyship identity is important to him, but it doesn't come across in an overbearing way. I thought I would begin this final chapter by recounting Tim's entire journey through the allyship pathway, step by step.

As with several of the men profiled in this book, Tim's journey started from the adversarial end of the starting-position spectrum. In Tim's words, he grew up with a "strong theology rooted in the hierarchy embedded in the Trinity."[1] Practically, in Tim's church experience, women were not allowed to lead in any way in the church service, and a good number of the women in Tim's church wore head coverings.[2]

---

[1]There has been considerable debate in recent years about whether there is in fact hierarchy embedded in the Trinity. Many complementarian theologians have posited such, with God the Father functioning as the ultimate authority and with Jesus and the Spirit in subordinate roles. Tim's church predicated its theological understanding of male headship on this way of comprehending the Trinity. In contrast, many egalitarian theologians have advocated for a Trinity marked by total mutuality. The most recent scholarship pushes against the idea that there are hierarchical relationships within the Trinity. Noting that the "hierarchical ordering of the three divine persons is a denial of the creeds and confessions of the church," Kevin Giles states, "The complementarian hierarchical doctrine of the Trinity now has few supporters. It has been abandoned even by many of its once most ardent supporters and advocates." Giles, *The Rise and Fall of the Complementarian Doctrine of the Trinity* (Cascade Books, 2017), 2-3.

[2]It would have been customary for women to cover their heads in the first-century church. Commenting on the text about head coverings in 1 Corinthians 11:2-16, Craig Keener writes: "Women's hair was a common object of lust in antiquity, and in much of the eastern

In terms of his experience at home, Tim's father, a local businessman, was militant in his practice of the Billy Graham rule, in one case choosing to only hire male personnel so that he would never have to meet one-on-one with a woman.[3] In addition, Tim's parents discouraged his sisters from going off to college upon graduating from high school, preferring instead that they take a gap year "in order to learn to sew and cook." Without a doubt, for Tim, a complementarian way of thinking and acting was "part of the air [they] breathed" as a family.

In our interview, Tim identified three specific disruptive encounters he had had with the notion of male privilege. The first disruptive encounter Tim faced came when he got to college and experienced firsthand the effective leadership of women in his campus ministry community. There were a number of women who were exercising able leadership when Tim got involved, but a woman named Lara stands out for Tim. Lara was directing the ministry, and Tim remembers watching her use her leadership gifts and thinking, *Wow, is that okay for her to be leading?* Given

---

Mediterranean women were expected to cover their hair. To fail to cover their hair was thought to provoke male lust as a bathing suit is thought to provoke it in some cultures today. Head covering prevailed in Jewish Palestine (where it extended even to a face veil) and elsewhere, but upper-class women eager to show off their fashionable hairstyles did not practice it. Thus Paul must address a clash of culture in the church between upper-class fashion and lower-class concern that sexual propriety is being violated." Paul's aim, then, was to address a particular issue endemic to the church in Corinth, but that hasn't stopped some Christians, including some collection of women from Tim's childhood church, from literally applying the words of 1 Corinthians 11 regarding head coverings in today's church setting as a way to demonstrate their belief in male headship. Keener, *The IVP Bible Background Commentary: New Testament* (IVP Academic, 1993), 475.

[3]Iconic evangelist Billy Graham's ministry was governed by a set of self-articulated rules, including one particular rule that has become ubiquitous in church culture around the world. In an effort to avoid a moral failure or even the appearance of a moral failure, Graham was systemically removed from any woman who wasn't his wife, Ruth. This is the practice Tim's father enthusiastically embraced as a model. In my research on thriving mixed-gender ministry partnerships, I concluded, "A rigid adherence to the Billy Graham Rule only hinders mixed-gender partnerships from flourishing." Instead of a blanket embrace of this generic boundary, I propose a contextualized approach to establishing boundaries in the context of women and men partnering together in ministry. Rob Dixon, *Together in Ministry: Women and Men in Flourishing Partnerships* (IVP Academic, 2021), 128.

his adversarial starting position, Lara's example of effective leadership was disorienting for Tim, but after observing her leadership, he became committed to exploring the "uneven playing field" that meant, "As a man, when I speak people will assume that I'm intelligent and that I have something to say . . . but a woman, on the other hand, it's pretty much assumed she has nothing to say."

In another example of a disruptive encounter, Tim remembers a woman named Sharon preaching at a conference on the topic of sin, and her message "reshaped my whole worldview of the Bible, people, and everything else. . . . It was the best talk on sin that I had ever heard. Both the content of her message and the fact that she was the one doing the preaching bent me. How could the Holy Spirit bless someone who was so blatantly in sin?" This experience of hearing a woman preach with insight and power was disruptive for Tim in a fundamentally personal way.

A third disruptive encounter came during a conversation Tim had with his female supervisor, Rose. At one point she shared with him a story about how a man had taken credit for an idea a female colleague had put forward. In response Tim expressed his outrage, and then he asked Rose whether she had ever seen him do anything like that. Her response? "Yeah, you have." That moment was a "huge eye opener" for Tim, because it caused him to realize that "my experience of myself and others' experience of me can be so different, and that men can do these things and not even know what they are doing."

These three disruptive encounters were challenging for Tim, but thankfully he responded well to them in step three. Following that initial experience of being surprised by Lara's effective leadership, Tim doubled down on placing himself under the leadership of a woman, and ultimately Lara mentored him for two years. After his experience with Sharon's authoritative teaching, Tim immersed himself in Bible study, exploring an egalitarian reading of the

Scriptures that provided a rationale for women using their gifts in this way. That focused study helped Tim to make his theological pivot. And following that disruptive conversation with Rose, Tim became a privilege detective, committing himself to not claiming credit from his colleagues by paying more attention to his participation in group settings, as an "act of repentance."

Once he was convinced about the reality of male privilege as well as the efficacy of an egalitarian reading of the Scriptures, Tim entered step four eager to express allyship with women in his ministry context. In one instance, in his first year of full-time vocational ministry, Tim appointed several women into leadership in the community he was leading, thus using the advocate role. That began what has become a career-long effort to identify and then raise up women into leadership. In addition, Tim channeled his allyship activities into writing. Taking what he had learned from his personal study as well as his experiences conducting theological seminars in various settings, Tim sat down and wrote an article laying out his egalitarian understanding. This article has endured, becoming an oft-used resource in his ministry context.[4]

Step five is the pushback step, and Tim is no stranger to pushback because of his male allyship. As noted, Tim's home church was very hostile to women in leadership, but the church was also financially supporting Tim's ministry, which included Tim's wife, Kathy. At one point, Tim's supervisor encouraged him to approach the church to see whether they would increase their financial contributions. Tim reached out to the elders and made the ask, and the church agreed, becoming Tim's biggest single donor. A year or two later, Kathy was promoted into leadership, and Tim became her second-in-command.

[4]Writing this article meant Tim was using the champion allyship role, because an article is designed for a wide audience.

When Tim's home church caught wind of this change, they called him and expressed concern with the arrangement. Months later, Tim spent a day with the elder team arguing for an egalitarian reading of the Scriptures. The elders were unconvinced, labeling Tim's perspective "unbiblical." According to Tim, it was a "huge time of tension." Because of the disagreement, Tim ultimately offered to withdraw from the church's support team, and the elders gratefully took him up on that offer. Pushback can be costly for would-be male allies, and it certainly was for Tim. The experience cost Tim a lot of funding, and it damaged Tim's relationships with several of the people at the church.

Perhaps the most compelling part of Tim's interview was when he discussed the things he has done over the years to invest in his identity as an ally as a part of his journey through step six. For instance, Tim has "wrestled with the Lord" about taking on more behind-the-scenes leadership roles. In one case, Kathy was invited to be the primary speaker at a conference while Tim was asked to do intercession, a "serve in the back room" kind of role. At first, Tim received this invitation as a slight, lamenting that he wouldn't be at the center of the conference experience. Tim "hated that and it rankled, because I was used to having those kinds of roles." Ultimately, after processing and praying, Tim realized, "If that's what it takes for a woman to be successful as a leader, to have an intercessor supporting her, I will embrace and accept that." Additionally, Tim has been proactive about investing in his allyship using the scholar role. Years ago, Tim committed to alternating his reading list between "WASP writers and women and people of color."[5]

Tim is now firmly in step seven, and like Lamar from chapter seven, he sees "training men to become allies" as a part of his

[5]In this case, it the acronym should actually be "WASPM," because Tim would include "male" alongside "white, Anglo-Saxon, and Protestant."

ministry calling. Accordingly, he routinely offers seminars on women in leadership, creating space for men to walk the same theological road he did years ago. In addition, he is purposeful about helping the men under his care to become aware of the adverse gender dynamics that can marginalize women. Like Rose did with him, Tim is focused on helping men "bring those negative dynamics to the surface." Finally, Tim is earnest about mentoring the men under his care to be proactive about developing women in their contexts into leaders.

All in all, Tim's allyship journey has been a joyous one. Even with the pushback he's encountered along the way, Tim loves being an ally. When I asked him how he feels about the term *ally*, he said with enthusiasm, "I embrace it!" To return once more to our composite definition of a male ally, Tim embodies the identity of a man who is engaged in an active process of understanding his privilege and empathetically seeking to leverage that privilege to benefit women both interpersonally and systemically.

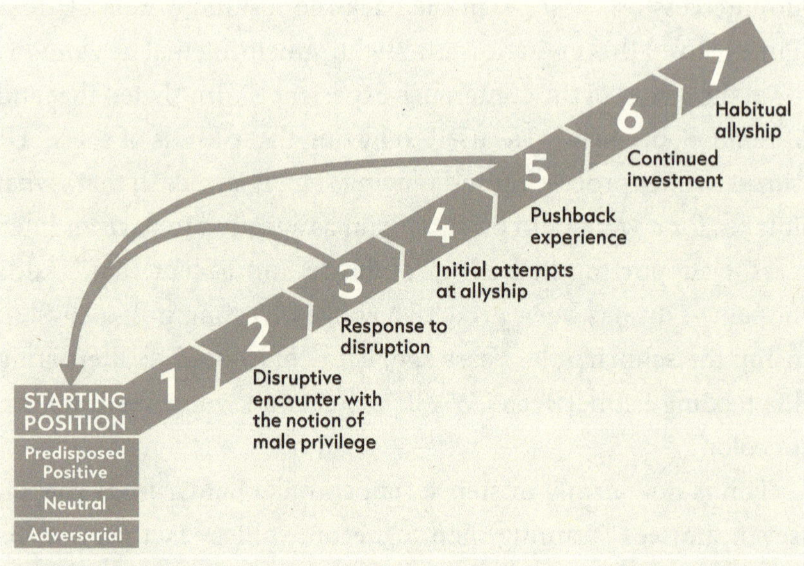

Figure 8.1. Allies in ministry developmental pathway
Design credit to my dear friend (and a legitimate male ally) Adam Loveridge.

THREE PLACES TO FOCUS

This book is about equipping more men to walk the allyship pathway Tim has walked and is continuing to walk. In pursuit of that goal, I want to delineate three strategic places where faith communities can invest in the project of developing more men into more effective allies to women in ministry. Applying intentional focus on these three places in the allyship pathway should result in more men like Tim engaged in our faith communities.

Creating disruptive encounters. First, faith communities can be intentional about crafting disruptive encounters for men in their midst. As noted in chapter two, sometimes disruptive encounters with the notion of male privilege just happen, but they can also be proactively engineered to engage men as they begin their journeys along the allyship pathway. Chapter two articulated a number of different examples of disruptive encounters, but I will offer three concrete stories here.

Convicted by its desire to empower women, one church decided to create a sermon series focused on Jesus as an ally to women. In terms of content, the church explored many of the texts referenced in chapter four. The choice to preach on this topic had several ripple effects. For one thing, women in the congregation were encouraged as they were reminded each week that Jesus cares for them. Without question, this church gave the women in their community a great gift. For another, men who were predisposed positive to the notion of male allyship were affirmed in their convictions and inspired to live them out more fully. On the other hand, for some women and men, the sermon series was supremely disruptive. These congregants had their views of women in leadership challenged, and the pastoral staff quickly realized they would need to create safe spaces for their folks to process their experiences on Sunday morning. Ultimately, while a few people left the church following the sermon series, many more entered into a process that yielded fruit in terms of newfound convictions about empowering women in ministry, including many men stepping onto the allyship pathway for the first time.

During the 2024 election cycle, there was a public conversation on the topic of masculinity as a part of a larger attempt by both parties to woo male voters. At issue was whether manhood has to be marked by strength, assertiveness, aggressiveness, and other trappings of traditional American masculinity.[6] Leveraging the public nature of the debate, one of my pastor friends decided to host a study group for men in his church to examine how Jesus might define masculinity. They carefully examined how Jesus expresses his masculinity in the Gospels, and they read *Malestrom* by Carolyn Custis James.[7] The experience functioned as a disruptive encounter for the men in the group. Indeed, as the group

---

[6]By and large, Democrats argued for an updated brand of masculinity, one in which men are able to be stereotypically masculine, if that's what suits them, but also one in which men could be ardent supporters of women and issues relevant to women. The choice of Minnesota Governor Tim Walz as Kamala Harris's running mate was designed to function as an avatar for this vision. In one video, Walz was seen fixing his truck; in the next, he was advocating for a woman's right to choose. In contrast, most Republicans pushed for a traditional version of masculinity, one that celebrated strength and power. In fact, "Trump and his campaign frequently [took] aim at Walz, calling him 'Tampon Tim'—a nickname stemming from a mischaracterization of a Minnesota law that requires schools to provide menstrual products in student restrooms. Trump boosters . . . also mocked Walz's masculinity online, seeking to block inroads with persuadable men." In perhaps the most vivid demonstration of the Republican Party's vision for masculinity, candidate Donald Trump was introduced at the Republican National Convention by none other than Hulk Hogan, an iconic professional wrestler who proceeded to rip his shirt off on stage. That Hogan struggled with the process was deemed ironic by many. Allan Smith, "Trump and Harris Battle over Male Voters—and What Masculinity Looks Like in 2024," NBC News, September 29, 2024, www.nbcnews.com/politics/2024-election/trump-harris-battle-male-voters-masculinity-2024-rcna173031.

[7]Carolyn Custis James, *Malestrom: How Jesus Dismantles Patriarchy and Redefines Manhood* (Zondervan, 2022). *Malestrom* is certainly an excellent read for a book group such as this, but other books could fit the bill as well, including Nate Pyle, *Man Enough: How Jesus Redefines Manhood* (Zondervan, 2015); Jared Yates Sexton, *The Man They Wanted Me to Be: Toxic Masculinity and a Crisis of Our Own Making* (Counterpoint, 2019); and Kristin Kobes Du Mez, *Jesus and John Wayne: How White Evangelicals Corrupted a Faith and Fractured a Nation* (Liveright, 2020).

came to a close, each man could articulate one specific way in which their focused study had reshaped his view of masculinity. Further, each man emerged with ideas about tangible ways he could better model his own personal masculinity around Jesus' example in the Gospels.

I teach leadership classes at my local Christian university, and one thing I'm intentional about is creating disruptive encounters for men in the context of our class's exploration of leadership and power. In particular, I have students read Mary Kate Morse's excellent book *Making Room for Leadership*.[8] Morse's contention in that book is that a person's relative level of social power can be determined by considering a wide range of social metrics, including gender. In Morse's rubric, men take up more social space in most settings in the American system. As a professor, it is always fascinating to watch men in my classes engage this reality. Some immediately push back, others embrace Morse's perspective either immediately or over time, and still others sit in thoughtful silence. Whatever their response, the common experience is disruption. I often hear male students express something along the lines of, "I've never thought about that before."[9]

As these three examples illustrate, disruptive encounters with the notion of male privilege can be proactively and thoughtfully programmed. This second step in the allyship pathway is one place that cries out for focused attention as faith communities go about developing more men into more effective allies to women in ministry. As churches consider designing disruptive encounters for men in their communities, reflection on the following questions can help:

---

[8]MaryKate Morse, *Making Room for Leadership: Power, Space and Influence* (InterVarsity Press, 2008).

[9]It should be noted that this stands in sharp contrast with the experience of female students, who almost uniformly tend to embrace Morse's words with vigor.

- Is the church's theology around women in leadership clear? Crafting disruptive encounters on this topic will be tougher if there is organizational or institutional ambiguity on this topic.
- Who are the men the church is wanting to impact? As noted in chapter one, a man's starting position is important. In some cases, it may work well to invite any and all men into a disruptive encounter around this topic, but in other instances it might be wise to be more selective, tailoring the encounter to a specific subset of men. A disruptive encounter designed for predisposed positive men might look very different from one designed for adversarial men.
- What resources does the church have to work with? As a general rule, churches should craft a disruptive encounter only if they can do it with excellence. For instance, thinking of the first story above, if there is no one who can preach a sermon series on the topic of male allyship with integrity, the church should probably hold off on using that structure as a disruptive encounter.
- How will the church execute the disruptive encounter? Churches should strive to be diligent in their preparation and execution.
- What is the follow-up plan? As important as the disruptive encounter is, the response to that experience matters more. The church mentioned above ventured into its disruptive encounter without a follow-up plan, and so it was forced to scramble to create one in real time. Ideally, the disruptive encounter would flow directly into a carefully planned time of response, and that takes work to create and articulate.

Again, some disruptive encounters just happen, while others can be thoughtfully crafted. Appointing a leader or a group of leaders to facilitate disruptive encounters for men in the congregation would be a great next step for a faith community to take in response to this book.

Guiding men through steps three and five. A second place for faith communities to focus is in mobilizing habitual allies to guide men through steps three and five. Since these are the two steps on the allyship pathway where men might opt out, it makes strategic sense to deploy process helpers as would-be male allies traverse them.

As noted in chapter three, disruptive encounters are useful only if men respond well to them, and for would-be male allies starting out on the allyship pathway, that response often requires process help from more-seasoned allies. Borrowing from chapter seven, habitual male allies can step in to mentor less-seasoned men through whatever dissonance is present in step three, sharing their own experiences to offer encouragement and support and exhorting them to continue along the allyship pathway.

Likewise, mentoring support can be crucial as would-be male allies navigate the pushback that comes during step five. I started chapter five with a story about a time I functioned as a process helper for Keith, a less-seasoned campus minister who had experienced pushback for the first time in response to his initial allyship attempts. If faith communities thoughtfully assign habitual male allies to guide men as they navigate step five, those men might well be more likely to remain on the allyship pathway, even in the face of a painful or dissonant experience.

I have personally been helped by habitual allies at step five on the pathway. In one case, a local pastor accused me of false teaching because I was permitting women to preach the Bible in our weekly fellowship meetings.[10] This experience was devastating for me as a would-be ally, but thankfully I had a more-seasoned mentor to help me through it. His guidance for me included walking me through my intense feelings of frustration and hurt, urging me to

---

[10]I tell this story more fully in my book on mixed-gender ministry partnerships, *Together in Ministry*, 50-51.

leverage the experience of disruption to work hard in my personal Bible study, and, when I ultimately became combative toward others who did not agree with my impulse to advocate for women in leadership, reminding me that I needed to become someone who could hold my convictions with humility.

Mentors have a crucial role to play in guiding would-be allies through these two steps on the pathway. Being purposeful about linking seasoned allies with up-and-coming ones is one important place to focus as faith communities seek to develop more men into more effective allies to women in ministry. Further, as I wrote in chapter seven, an allyship cohort could be an effective vehicle for mentors to guide less-seasoned men through these two steps as well.

Celebrating the wins. A third place for faith communities to focus is on celebrating male allies as they experience wins along the pathway. Generally speaking, celebrating wins is an important step for both individuals and communities. Writing in the *Harvard Business Review*, Whitney Johnson notes,

> Celebration is an important opportunity to cement the lessons learned on the path to achievement, and to strengthen the relationships between people that make future achievement more plausible. Celebration is an event, not a destination. It's the little pause where we survey the road we've traveled and the mountain we've climbed. We can have a snack, with our colleagues or friends, rather than alone in our office. We rest, we catch our breath, we contemplate the next opportunity ahead, before descending to climb again. But the fact that the interval is brief doesn't make it unimportant, or harmless if neglected. Celebrating achievements great and small is high octane fuel for further achievement. We don't just celebrate the win; we celebrate *to* win.[11]

[11] Whitney Johnson, "Celebrate to Win," *Harvard Business Review*, January 26, 2022, https://hbr.org/2022/01/celebrate-to-win.

In chapter seven, I referenced the male allyship cohort I put together with a group of men from my ministry context. And I noted that I did two things to share the cohort with our larger leadership team. First, before we started, I asked permission from the key women in our ministry context, including our supervisor. This was an important move, as it gained buy-in from the larger community and particularly from women in our community. Second, I made an announcement at the end of the cohort designed to celebrate these men and their investment in developing as allies. Each of these moves was useful in both building ownership for the cohort across our team and deepening the value for male allyship in our community.

Still, looking back, I wish I had done more. In particular, I wish I had carved out space in a subsequent team meeting to really celebrate the win the cohort represented. I could have had the men involved share testimonies about what they learned and how the cohort experience shaped them. I could have had senior women in our community come forward to bless and commission these men into their allyship. And I could have used the opportunity to exhort other men to step up as allies, perhaps even announcing another round of the male allyship cohort. As Johnson notes above, there is something about a robust and public affirmation that cements a value in a community's life together.

My hope in writing *Allies in Ministry* has been to encourage individual men to progress along the allyship pathway on their way to becoming habitual allies. Individual responses are certainly important, but so are communal ones. I hope faith communities can become experts in crafting disruptive encounters, devising support systems for men navigating both step three and step five, and celebrating the wins as God develops more men into more effective allies to women in context.

WE CAN DO THIS!

My friend Angel got ordained recently. What a moment of triumph, as her pastors testified that both her calling and gifting aligned with the ongoing ministry of the church.

As precious as it was, this ordination milestone was merely the culmination of more than twenty years of faithful ministry service for Angel. Her ministry journey started during her college years as she strove to help her peers experience more of Jesus in their lives. Then it continued into urban ministry, where she worked her way up in an organization devoted to community development work, ultimately becoming the organization's CEO. Next, she ventured into church ministry, pouring into the next generation of students and families. Through each of her ministry phases, Angel has brought her undeniable preaching gift, her passion for social justice, and her relentless quest to help others embrace God's love for the whole world. Without question, Angel repeatedly exhibited a track record of quality ministry; because of that, becoming ordained was merely a formal endorsement of her years of faithful and effective ministry work.

At the same time, when I look at Angel's ministry journey, I can see the contributions of male allies. There's the male hiring supervisor who used the champion and sponsor roles to appoint Angel into her first leadership position. There's a subsequent male supervisor who used the upstander, amplifier, and sponsor roles to promote her in their organization. There's the male leader from outside her organization who saw her gifting and passion and used the confidant and scholar roles to further round out Angel's leadership skills. And then there's the nationally known male leader who used the advocacy role in making space in his up-and-coming leader's cohort for Angel to join. In a very real way, these men and others helped usher Angel through her leadership journey.

The point of this story is not to lionize these men. Their choices to adopt these various allyship roles are commendable, but this story is about Angel, a woman who is a gift to the church and to God's mission. What these allies did is to help make the gift that is Angel just a bit easier for the church to receive. In the process, they faithfully fulfilled our working definition of a male ally as a man who is engaged in an active process of understanding his privilege and empathetically seeking to leverage that privilege to benefit women both interpersonally and systemically.

As I was writing this book, I found myself in a back-and-forth with a seminary student who found my *Priscilla Papers* article online and wanted to dialogue about its contents. In particular, he was making the case that one of the dangers embedded in the notion of male allyship is centering the male ally at the expense of the women he is seeking to serve. He identified the concern as the "male savior complex," concluding with this note: "The only ally women need is Jesus."

I can agree that ultimately Jesus is the ally women need. As I have demonstrated in this book, Jesus was (and is) a consistent and generous ally to women. And any attempt for men to emulate Jesus as an ally will rely on Jesus' power and direction.

On the other hand, it seems incomplete to me to simply say that Jesus is the only ally women need. Because what if, in this season of the church's life and ministry, Jesus chooses to express his allyship through a cadre of developed and mobilized male allies? What if one of Jesus' strategies for building a church where women and men can thrive together in mutuality is men's adopting the identity of an ally, thereby functioning as sub-allies with Jesus as their guide?

In today's church, we desperately need more Tims to make it possible for the Angels in our midst to shine in the way God has intended them to. May the pathway articulated in this book inspire us all to partner with Jesus in developing more men into more effective allies to women in ministry.

QUESTIONS FOR REFLECTION

- What could it look like for your faith community to proactively and intentionally create disruptive encounters for the men in your community?
- Who are the seasoned male allies in your faith community who could become mentors to less-seasoned men as they traverse both the disruptive-encounter and pushback steps on the pathway?
- What could it look like for your community to celebrate the wins by publicly affirming men who successfully navigate the allyship pathway?
- Overall, how has this book helped you to think about the topic of male allyship?
- What further questions do you have about the topic of male allyship, and where can you go to get them answered?
- What could it look like for you to use this content to develop more male allies in your context? What are your concrete next steps?

ACKNOWLEDGMENTS

WRITING A BOOK IS HARD WORK. It's wonderful work, particularly if, like me, you are more than passionate about your topic, but it's hard work. And so I'm grateful for the many friends and partners who stood beside me as I've labored toward bringing *Allies in Ministry* into the world.

First, thanks to the many men who participated in my research study. Your stories and insights represent the beating heart of the allyship pathway! In the interest of confidentiality, I won't name names here, but if I had a chat with you about this topic at some point in the last several years, know that you have fueled this book and that I'm full of gratitude for each one of you.

Thanks also to my writing support team, the self-labeled #bookdoulas. You helped me deliver my first book, and I'm so thankful you returned for a second round in the literary delivery room. I appreciate the prayers, texts of encouragement, and silly GIFs along the way. To Nicole, Matt, Layla, and Todd, thank you. Can't wait for the next book!

I owe a debt to the many folks from my vocational worlds who have helped me make space to imagine, create, edit, and promote this book. Thanks to Anne, Eddy, and Greg on the InterVarsity side. Thanks also to my advocates at Fresno Pacific University and Fuller Theological Seminary. And of course, thanks to the wonderful folks at InterVarsity Press, to my editors Jon Boyd and Rebecca

Carhart-Mader, and to all of the saints who have worked behind the scenes to bring *Allies in Ministry* into being.

And then I certainly need to honor my family, who have been invested in this book along with me. Amy, thanks for being a sounding board and giving me space to verbally process, particularly when I ran into some sort of conundrum. Josh, Lucy, Gracie, and Lily (and Clementine!), thanks for giving your father space to write. With this book, I'm now just two books behind your mom!

Finally, I dedicate *Allies in Ministry* to the memory of Garrett Girard. Garrett was a dear friend, and I miss him terribly. Garrett would resonate with the theme of this book, as he was a faithful ally to the women in his life, including his wife, Amy, their two daughters, and many other women who crossed his path, including women in church leadership. As I've gone about my writing, I've truly missed Garrett's editorial eye. He was the very first person to read my previous book, *Together in Ministry*, and I felt his loss in writing the book you now hold in your hands. Rest in peace, dear friend. And go Lakers!

GENERAL INDEX

SCRIPTURE INDEX

ALSO BY THE AUTHOR

Together in Ministry
978-1-5140-0070-0

Penny Preaches
978-1-5140-0858-4

Missio Alliance

Missio Alliance has arisen in response to the shared voice of pastors and ministry leaders from across the landscape of North American Christianity for a new "space" of togetherness and reflection amid the issues and challenges facing the church in our day. We are united by a desire for a fresh expression of evangelical faith, one significantly informed by the global evangelical family. Lausanne's Cape Town Commitment, "A Confession of Faith and a Call to Action," provides an excellent guidepost for our ethos and aims.

Through partnerships with schools, denominational bodies, ministry organizations, and networks of churches and leaders, Missio Alliance addresses the most vital theological and cultural issues facing the North American church in God's mission today. We do this primarily by convening gatherings, curating resources, and catalyzing innovation in leadership formation.

Rooted in the core convictions of evangelical orthodoxy, the ministry of Missio Alliance is animated by a strong and distinctive theological identity that emphasizes

Comprehensive Mutuality: Advancing the partnered voice and leadership of women and men among the beautiful diversity of the body of Christ across the lines of race, culture, and theological heritage.

Hopeful Witness: Advancing a way of being the people of God in the world that reflects an unwavering and joyful hope in the lordship of Christ in the church and over all things.

Church in Mission: Advancing a vision of the local church in which our identity and the power of our testimony is found and expressed through our active participation in God's mission in the world.

In partnership with InterVarsity Press, we are pleased to offer a line of resources authored by a diverse range of theological practitioners. The resources in this series are selected based on the important way in which they address and embody these values, and thus, the unique contribution they offer in equipping Christian leaders for fuller and more faithful participation in God's mission.

missioalliance.org | twitter.com/missioalliance | facebook.com/missioalliance

Dr. Rob Dixon is ready to help you think about male allyship as well as the caliber of mixed-gender ministry partnerships in your church, community, or organization. Using almost three decades of campus ministry experience with InterVarsity Christian Fellowship and a training model developed during his doctoral studies at Fuller Theological Seminary, Rob is available for coaching, consulting, and training on a range of topics at the intersection of gender and faith.

Rob is a senior fellow with the InterVarsity Institute. The Institute exists to provide consulting, coaching, and training experiences for leaders and organizations to help them achieve their mission by reflecting biblical values in the areas of race, gender, and sexuality.

Want your value for gender equality to better match your practice?
Let Dr. Dixon help!

To reach Rob and set up an appointment, go to **https://intervarsity.org/institute** and click on the orange "Contact Us" button at the bottom of the page.

www.ingramcontent.com/pod-product-compliance
Lightning Source LLC
LaVergne TN
LVHW050959080826
845145LV00009B/2361

* 9 7 8 1 5 1 4 0 1 2 5 8 1 *